1

Deeper Bible Thinking

by Charles O. Young, Ph.D.

Printed in the United States of America
ISBN-13 978-0615779355

Table of Contents

Prologue --6

Blessed--9

Sovereignty ---17

Predestination --34

Why Does God Allow Evil ------------------------------------40

Prophecy ---53

Religion ---65

Repentance--80

Baptism Regeneration --97

Speaking in Tongues---128

Storehouse Tithing ---158

Lordship Salvation ---180

Divorce and Remarriage--------------------------------------198

To Drink or Not to Drink – Alcohol ----------------------216

The Homosexual Discussion --------------------------------249

Shorts ---265

Prologue

Over the years I have held views of certain doctrines that have made me uncomfortable. From my education - both formal and informal - I have found many doctrinal ideas that have more than one view. It is these doctrines that probably end up forming denominations. Even within denominations; interpretations change. I also find that interpretations often change with *individuals* as circumstances change.

In an effort to satisfy my own theology, I have spent time both researching Scripture and pondering. My method of consideration was to take a giant step backward to get a bigger picture. Instead of becoming immersed in the minutia of the theology, I tried to see the bigger picture. I tried to ask better questions. For instance, in the section about Storehouse Tithing, instead of trying to figure out the difference between law and grace, I asked "Why is storehouse tithing indefensible in the New Testament?" It allowed me to grasp an idea that I had not before considered. You will understand when you visit that section.

This book contains a handful of the troublesome matters that have bothered me for decades, but is not by any means the end of my own theological curiosity. It is not important that anyone agrees with my conclusions. My only goal is to satisfy own lack of understanding. You must either go through the same process yourself or blindly accept everything that you have been taught. Prepare to think!

Blessed

Are you blessed? Have you *been* blessed? Are you *being* blessed? What does it *mean* to be blessed?

There is a certain truth taught throughout Scripture that is clearly stated in James 1:17, "Every good gift and every perfect gift is from above, and comes down from the Father of lights, with whom there is no variation or shadow of turning." God is the source of blessing. *Blessing* really feels good, doesn't it? Everyone likes to believe that God has shown him some special favor. Over the years, however, I have recognized that sometimes blessing does NOT feel good. Sometimes it hurts.

Recently while teaching in an underground seminary in a Muslim country, I asked my opening "blessing" questions to the 20 Arab believers who were in the class. The answers that I received centered on God giving special favor to an individual. The men to whom I was speaking did not seem to have much of the blessings of God. All of them had been ostracized by their families and their own communities because of their recent "conversion" to becoming followers of Jesus. Some of them were even forced to live on the street, wondering where they would get their next meal. These men did not feel blessed. They felt beat down, persecuted, maybe even forsaken by God. How does the idea of "blessing" equate with *these* men?

Today, in our American society, the word "blessed" is bantered about almost carelessly. It is used to draw people into church or to interest them in the things of God. It is certainly a draw to seekers trying to figure out how God works and what would be the benefit of having a relationship with Him. Everyone *wants* to be blessed. Books have been written, slogans have been developed and songs are sung to try to generate a positive attitude about God. I too have used the word often to influence people into seeking God through Jesus, for the Kingdom.

My favorite Psalm is Psalm 1. It starts with "Blessed is the man who ..." then a description of the favor shown to the blessed man. He will be strong, he will flourish, and he will bear fruit. Joshua 1:8 is my favorite verse in the entire Bible, it ends with "... then you shall make your way prosperous, then you shall have good success." It seems clear to me that God wants to favor His people, God wants to pour out blessings on certain people, that God wants to open the windows of Heaven to people, but I don't think that God blesses simply for the sake of blessing. In fact, one reason given for God's blessing in Psalm 67:1-2 is for the furtherance of the Gospel, *"God be merciful to us and bless us, and cause His face to shine upon us, Selah ² That Your way may be known on earth, Your salvation among all nations."* Israel *failed* to spread the good news of God and God removed His hand of blessing from them, Matthew 21:43,

10

"Therefore I say to you, the kingdom of God will be taken from you and given to a nation bearing the fruits of it."

The problem as I see it is trying to define "blessed," to determine what generates a blessing, and to recognize blessing as it happens. Imagine the damage that can be done if a person *"needs"* a blessing and does not receive it. What if someone needs healing and does not receive it? What if a family is about to lose their home and God doesn't provide resources to pay for it? I think that the health of Christianity in our country may be linked to the disappointment felt by those who have their *"needs"* unmet by God.

One thing that I see evidenced in the Bible is that God faithfully demonstrates how He works with mankind. The model of interaction can be seen as a father/son relationship. How would a proper father deal with his child? I recognize that some people have no frame of reference because of a failed relationship with their own father, but imagine the *spiritual* relationship as a perfect union. Hebrews 12 is a very interesting portion of Scripture that demonstrates this relationship,

> [5] *"And you have forgotten the exhortation which speaks to you as to sons: "My son, do not despise the chastening of the LORD, Nor be discouraged when you are rebuked by Him;* [6] *For whom the LORD loves He chastens, And scourges every son*

11

whom He receives." [7] *If you endure chastening, God deals with you as with sons; for what son is there whom a father does not chasten?* [8] *But if you are without chastening, of which all have become partakers, then you are illegitimate and not sons.* [9] *Furthermore, we have had human fathers who corrected us, and we paid them respect. Shall we not much more readily be in subjection to the Father of spirits and live?* [10] *For they indeed for a few days chastened us as seemed best to them, but He for our profit, that we may be partakers of His holiness.* [11] *Now no chastening seems to be joyful for the present, but painful; nevertheless, afterward it yields the peaceable fruit of righteousness to those who have been trained by it."*

The payoff of spiritual discipline is found in verse 11. Its purpose as stated is to yield something, the peaceable fruit of righteousness. The cause of this discipline is found in verse 6, God loves us. Is there "blessing" found in this passage? I think yes. The blessing is that God loves us and that He loves us too much to allow us not to grow. His purpose, as with any proper father, is to love us and grow us. That's *blessing*.

I am not asserting that every trial that comes from God is some sort of punishment. I *am* suggesting that God is constantly involved in our lives to create in us "discipline," - spiritual discipline. Years ago there was a movie called "The Karate Kid." The "kid" was mentored by an old karate veteran who taught him the skills necessary to become a karate expert. Early on, the veteran sent the kid out to clean up all of the cars on the lot. He taught him the physical technique to "properly" wax the cars. While moving his hands and arms in a circular motion, the old gent would say with one motion "wax on" and with the opposite motion "wax off." The kid did not know that he was learning karate motions that were necessary to become competent in karate. He was gaining strength in each arm that would serve him in his karate career. The pain of the work paid off for him later when he was accosted by his karate adversary.

Our misconception is that "blessing" always feels good. We all love blessings that provide for our needs, give peace, and that feel good. I have experienced blessings in my life that I deemed to be directly from the hand of God. However, I do wonder sometimes if God gets credit for blessing when there was nothing special intended by God. The Bible tells us that the rain falls on the just and the unjust, Matthew 5:45. Is that just the law of nature at work? (More on that later.) The discipline mentioned in Hebrews 12 is designed to create in believers, discipline — discipline in overcoming the flesh, discipline in prayer, discipline in growth, discipline in work, discipline in authority, and discipline in curbing our naturally lazy and unconcerned self-interests.

If a father did not instill in his children these normal disciplines, they would certainly live unproductive lives. In fact, the Bible says that if a father does not discipline his children, he hates them (Proverbs 13:24). Jails are full of people who have lived undisciplined lives. Welfare rolls are crowded with people who live undisciplined lives. Why is there so much drug abuse in America? Why is there so much "get rich quick" crime? You can see where this is going?

My father became a follower of Jesus when I was 13 years old. He immediately put me on a spiritual path that was very uncomfortable. He sent me to a Christian school. He forced me to go to church. He tried the best that he could to start me down a path that was unfamiliar to me and certainly unwelcomed. I resisted every step of the way. Surely he had gone mad. That path, as unwanted as it was, has created in me a much needed relationship with God, launched me into a lifetime of ministry, and sent me around the world sharing the same message of God that I had so fervently resisted. For me, he did it right.

The same process is true from a spiritual standpoint. Without God discipling us, we would be carnal, selfish, self-centered, prayerless, lazy, unconcerned, uninformed and certainly

14

unproductive at the spiritual level. One blessing is that God *will* try to shape believers away from being carnal flesh satisfiers. In most adult Sunday School classes we share prayer requests. One overweight person requests that God will miraculously bless him by healing his diabetes. Perhaps the prayer should be that we don't eat so many Twinkies. We pray for the person who has overextended himself and bought too many new cars and now can't make the house payments. What should the prayer be?

Whom the Lord loves he disciplines

Though life is full of all kinds of blessings, THAT to me is the ultimate blessing. God's discipline creates God's disciples. Discipline is not necessarily punishment. One can however learn a lot from hunger, pain, loss, and overall lack. Salvation costs you nothing. Discipleship costs you everything. Perhaps my friends in the North African underground seminary are more blessed than we are. We all need spiritual strength to succeed against the adversary. Wax on, wax off.

Sovereignty

Objectivity is very subjective.

Several years ago, while teaching a doctrinal lesson to a group of men, I was challenged about my position on the matter. The challenger asked me if he could present an opposing view the next week. I agreed. The next week he made his presentation. I was quite struck that he used the same Scripture references to prove his position that I had used the week before. Our positions were quite opposed to each other.

It became apparent to me that the use of Scripture is a complicated matter. A person can use the Scripture to prove any doctrine that he deems correct. Usually he will support the doctrine in which he grew up. It's rare that a person will change his position on any given biblical doctrine. The only people who *can* be influenced are new believers. Even *they* are likely to adopt the doctrine of their mentor. I'm quite sure that all I just wrote applies to me also. Over the years I have asked myself questions that have helped me clarify some ideas but have rarely changed them. With so many ideas floating around, this is my attempt to analyze Scripture on the subject of sovereignty.

The Big Question

The question at hand is "how much does God intervene in your life?" Does He control your life? Does He manage your life? Does He cause bad things to happen? I find that the answer to the matter is a moving target. With every major event, many believers fall back to the position that "God is in charge, He knows what He is doing." This to me is an oversimplified feel good mind-set. It tries to make God fit into our lives but ignores us fitting into His purpose. This introduces the word "sovereignty." The word sovereignty does not appear in the King James Bible but the concept is all over it. Sovereignty denotes the highest power or authority. Sovereign suggests that there is no power greater than THE power. Throughout the Bible, the supreme authority of God is clearly taught. In Psalm 40 God Himself declares His own power and authority. He is supreme, righteous, all knowing, all powerful, present everywhere at all times, eternal, able to do anything He wishes, has creative ability, foreknows all things, answers to no-one, is perfect by His own standard, loves completely, judges righteously and is only bound by His own word. He is THE power. He is THE authority.

Man's Will

Another very obvious aspect of Scripture is that there is a grand tension between God's will and man's will. In Genesis 2 God gave men a great gift, choice. Adam and Eve exercised this choice and even chose against God. They actually chose to follow the allure of Satan – Satan - the essence of evil, the presence of evil, the antithesis of God.

In Genesis chapters 1-3, I find a very interesting *unstated* premise; God is willing to *delegate* His authority. God created a magnificent perfect world, by His incredible sovereign power, then gave authority for it to man, even allowing man to choose against Him. What sovereignty! God delegated His power to Satan to allow him to influence man, even against God Himself. God set in motion a power that would curse man all of his days - nature or natural occurrences. The players then, in this drama of world events include: God, Satan, man, nature.

Natural Laws

Today we are certainly bound by the laws of nature. If you jump from a bridge, you will fall - maybe to your death. Remember, *death* was a result of the fall of man. If you run your car into a wall, you will crash - maybe even die. Today, it is clear that everything tends to wind down, degenerate, aka entropy. We all get old, our bodies fail and we die. All of these are the results of the fall even though they are quite "natural." Natural disasters occur all of the time as a result of God's sovereign power being delegated to "nature." In Florida, April is the driest month. Does

19

God have April dryness on His schedule to bring it to Florida? During the summer, we have "summertime weather patterns." Most evenings over central Florida, the air from the Gulf of Mexico collides with the air from the Atlantic. When combined with heat and moisture and we have storms around 4 p.m. Does God have to remember to schedule "summertime weather patterns?" June 1 through November 30 is called hurricane season. Natural occurrences happen during that season that brings hurricanes from western Africa, across the Atlantic Ocean, to the east coast of the Americas. It's natural. Together these phenomena are the results of the fall, man's original choice influenced by Satan, and granted by God. Of course, God can at any moment circumvent the laws of nature but generally does not. Man's activities are not restricted by God unless God chooses. Satan is not restrained by God unless God intervenes. In Job chapters 1 – 2, God allowed Satan to antagonize Job. Who was it that sent the whirl-wind to destroy Job's family? It wasn't God. The course of nature is not changed unless God, in His sovereignty, has a special purpose.

Why?

One question that I find missing as I study the many ideas about sovereignty is the question why. What is God's motivation? The extremes of predestination, aka sovereign election, assert that God chooses people for heaven and hell. I can't help but ask "why?" It would be like God playing chess with Himself. It's like playing a game with yourself and you already know which moves you will make and how it will turn out. What's the point? There must be another overarching purpose that God has in mind. My theory, though maybe not perfect, at least tries to make some sense of it all. We are taught in 1 John that "God is love." Jesus said in John 15 that the greatest level of love is demonstrated by one giving his life for another. If the highest level of love is to die for another, could God do any less? For whom would He die? Why would He die for an individual? Thus, God created man with a choice to fail, under the penalty of death. Did it ever occur to you that God invented death for the human experience? Have you ever wondered, "why death?" It is my assertion that God was compelled by love to die for another when he created man. How could He die if He did not *become* a man? It seems to me that God had an itch to scratch, love. Imagine perfect love floating through eternity with no place to land. If one can achieve the highest level of love by dying for another, God must *exceed* that level by dying for *all*.

Randomness

Now let's introduce the idea of randomness. If I choose to drive my car carelessly during a natural phenomenon -- "rain" -- I could easily run into the back of another car driven by a person who chose to suddenly stop because of a dog running across busy traffic. Would God cause that to happen? I say that it is an intersection of choices and natural events that caused the accident, not God. Was it with the permissive will of God? Of course! None of these would have happened had God not delegated His authority. God delegates but does not "manage" unless he has a special purpose in mind.

Special Purpose

Several times we have alluded to "special purpose." Does God have a special purpose or special program designed to get to the desired end - love man? One very obvious theme throughout Scripture is that God has chosen a group of people, Israel, through whom he can fulfill His purpose. By observing Israel one can learn about God, how He responds to sin, how He blesses, how He curses, and where He is going. All nations of the earth can be blessed to know God by observing Israel. That's a blessing! Israel was not only chosen to carry the message of God to the world, but is also predestined to once again carry the message, the next time declaring Jesus as the Messiah. The closer that a person lives to God's special purpose, the more of the hand of God can be seen in that life, Psalm. 67:1-2. This "special purpose" drives an enormous amount of Scripture and should be considered every time an interpretation is needed. Notice how Israel and this special purpose weave their way through difficult Scripture.

*12 Then Moses said to the LORD, "See, You say to me, 'Bring up **this** people.' But You have not let me know whom You will send with me. Yet You have said, 'I know you by name, and you have also found grace in My sight.' 13 Now therefore, I pray, if I have found grace in Your sight, show me now Your way, that I may know You and that I may find grace in Your sight. And consider that **this nation** is Your people."*

14 And He said, "My Presence will go with you, and I will give you rest."

*15 Then he said to Him, "If Your Presence does not go with us, do not bring us up from here. 16 For how then will it be known that **Your people** and I have found grace in Your sight, except You go with us? So we shall be separate, **Your people** and I, from all the people who are upon the face of the earth."*

17 So the LORD said to Moses, "I will also do this thing that you have spoken; for you have found grace in My sight, and I know you by name."

¹⁸ And he said, "Please, show me Your glory."

¹⁹ Then He said, "I will make all My goodness pass before you, and I will proclaim the name of the LORD before you. I will be gracious to whom I will be gracious, and I will have compassion on whom I will have compassion."

Notice that the above Scripture designates Israel as the recipient of this special treatment with a special purpose in mind - carrying the message of God to the entire world. Israel was chosen at this time to receive His mercy and compassion.

Romans 9

*⁶ But it is not that the word of God has taken no effect. For they are not all **Israel** who are of Israel, ⁷ nor are they all children because they are the seed of Abraham; but, "In Isaac your seed shall be called." ⁸ That is, those who are the children of the flesh, these are not the children of God; but the children **of the promise** are counted as the seed. ⁹ For this is the word of promise: "At this time I will come and Sarah shall have a son."*

¹⁰ And not only this, but when Rebecca also had

24

conceived by one man, even by our father Isaac *[11] (for the children not yet being born, nor having done any good or evil, that the* **purpose of God** *according to election might stand, not of works but of Him who calls),* *[12] it was said to her, "The older shall serve the younger."* *[13] As it is written, "Jacob I have loved, but Esau I have hated."* *[14] What shall we say then? Is there unrighteousness with God? Certainly not!* *[15] For He says to Moses, "I will have mercy on whomever I will have mercy, and I will have compassion on whomever I will have compassion."* *[16] So then it is not of him who wills, nor of him who runs, but of God who shows mercy.* *[17] For the Scripture says to the Pharaoh, "For this very* **purpose** *I have raised you up, that I may show My power in you, and that* **My name may be declared in all the earth."** *[18] Therefore He has mercy on whom He wills, and whom He wills He hardens.*

This passage is a simple restatement of the history found in Exodus 33. "Harden" does not consign a person to hell. The persons own choice does that. God had used a lost person to fulfill His special purpose.

25

Acts 13

*44 On the next Sabbath almost the whole city came together to hear the word of God. 45 But when the Jews saw the multitudes, they were filled with envy; and contradicting and blaspheming, they opposed the things spoken by Paul. 46 Then Paul and Barnabas grew bold and said, "It was necessary that the word of God should be spoken to you first; but since you reject it, and judge yourselves unworthy of everlasting life, behold, we turn to the Gentiles. 47 For so the Lord has commanded us: 'I have set you as a **light to the Gentiles**, That you should be for salvation to the **ends of the earth**.'" 48 Now when the Gentiles heard this, they were glad and glorified the word of the Lord. And as many as had been appointed to eternal life believed.*

Ephesians 1

1 Paul, an apostle of Jesus Christ by the will of God, To the saints who are in Ephesus, and faithful in Christ Jesus: 2 Grace to you and peace from God our Father and the Lord Jesus Christ. 3 Blessed be the God and Father of our Lord Jesus Christ, who has blessed us with every spiritual blessing in the heavenly places in Christ, ⁴just as He chose us in Him before the foundation of the world, that we should be holy and without blame before Him in love, ⁵having **predestined us to adoption as sons by Jesus Christ to Himself**, *according to the good pleasure of His will, ⁶to the praise of the glory of His grace, by which He made us accepted in the Beloved.*

I Peter 1

1 Peter, an apostle of Jesus Christ, To the **pilgrims of the Dispersion** *in Pontus, Galatia, Cappadocia, Asia, and Bithynia, ²elect according to the foreknowledge of God the Father, in sanctification of the Spirit, for obedience and sprinkling of the blood of Jesus Christ: Grace to you and peace be multiplied.*

Notice the purpose of God being extended to the Gentile world. Even though the nation of Israel nationally rejected the Messiah, God's purpose is not frustrated. If Israel had not rejected Him, we may not even know that Jesus existed. Peter had to justify his actions of including Cornelius, a gentile, in Acts 11 to the Jewish counsel in Jerusalem. Jesus may have remained a Jewish religious figure if it were not for the rejection. On the Road to

Emmaus, Luke 24, Jesus encountered two men who were wondering about the resurrection. God interrupted "nature" and managed the minds of the two travelers.

> Luke 24:16 "*16 But their eyes were restrained, so that they did not know Him.*"

If God had not "blinded" their minds, the conversation that followed would not have happened. It was an extremely important conversation, recorded for all man-kind, which greatly advanced the special purpose of God, as He validated the message by using prophecy. God is not about blinding men's minds, but this cause was great. This is a classic example of God working to His end.

Did God Know?

Foreknowledge, in 1 Peter 1 above, is an attribute of God not an act of God. If a person is *"elect according to the foreknowledge of God"*, God knew he would become a believer. By applying "foreknowledge" to some of the above Scriptures predestination tension can be softened. God certainly knew that Pharaoh in Romans 9 would not become a believer. With that knowledge God could harden Pharaoh's heart to accomplish His purpose of showing up all of the god's of Egypt for the whole world to observe. Each of the contests with Moses was designed to "conquer" one of the god's of Egypt. The "special purpose" of God was to demonstrate power over false gods, not to send Pharaoh to hell.

What is the will of God?

> 2 Peter 3:9 *" The Lord is not slack concerning His promises, as some count slackness, but is longsuffering toward us, not willing that any should perish but that all should come to repentance. "*

Can man's will trump God's will? It did in the following Scripture.

Matthew 23:37 *"O **Jerusalem, Jerusalem**, the one who kills the prophets and stones those who are sent to her! How often I wanted to gather your children together, as a hen gathers her chicks under her wings, but **you were not willing**! ³⁸ See! Your house is left to you desolate; ³⁹ for I say to you, you shall see Me no more till you say, 'Blessed is He who comes in the name of the LORD!' "*

Special Purpose

One of the most oft misquoted Scripture in the entire Bible is Jeremiah 29:11 *"¹¹ For I know the thoughts that I think toward you, says the LORD, thoughts of peace and*

29

not of evil, to give you a future and a hope."

I have ALWAYS heard this verse used by believers to make themselves feel good when something bad happens in their lives. To be honest with Scripture one must read the verse in context. Jeremiah 29: 10 makes it clear that God is talking to the southern kingdom of Israel, Judah. They were about to go into captivity for 70 years and God was talking to them as a nation, not personally. Shortly after this prophecy, Babylon marched against Judah, killing more than half of the people, taking the rest captive into Babylon.

What are the thoughts that God had/has for Judah? We know that answer as much as God wants us to know from reading the Scripture. It applies in large part to the nation of Israel. Here are some of the thoughts that God had/has for Israel. All of these were in the future of Israel as a nation. None of them were about any single person. This was a national statement.

Israel would go into captivity for 70 years
They would return to the land, rebuilding walls and city
They would reinstitute temple worship
The temple would be rebuilt
The nation would experience 400 years without a prophet
The divisive "religion" of Israel would be established
God Himself would become a man and enter the world

Jesus would die for all mankind

Israel as a nation would reject Jesus as the Messiah

Jesus would revoke God's blessing on Israel for a time

He would ascend into Heaven following commissioning

The Holy Spirit would descend and empower believers

The message of God would be spread

Jesus would come back receiving believers

Israel will "believe" as a nation

They will carry the message of God to all nations

Armageddon

Judgment

New Heaven and new earth

It is fairly simple to see the plans that God had/has when he spoke to Israel in Jeremiah 29. Sorry, Jeremiah 29:11 is not for you. Regardless of whether you are Jew or gentile (not Jew), we all fit into the special purpose of God. As we live our lives, we interact with the purpose of God. Sometimes we advance the purpose - sometimes not. God will lead us, challenge us, encourage us, and influence us as long as it advances His special purpose. He may even over-ride your will, restrain Satan or even overcome the laws of nature if it fits His purpose. The message of God will be spread to the world. Get on board!

How "in charge" is God?

The conclusion of this thesis is that God is sovereign. He has a plan in mind for man-kind. He probably has a plan in mind for you. You may or may not fill His purpose. He will not "manage" your life because He has delegated authority to you to manage your own. If asked, He will help you in your life but only to His purpose and His glory, not just for fun.

God can intervene any time He chooses, changing the laws of nature, constraining Satan and even directing your life, but He rarely does. God has predestined/chosen/ordained the nation of Israel to share the message of God through Jesus the Messiah to the entire world. All believers will be conformed to the image of Jesus one day. The only time that God "manages" one's life (Abraham, Jeremiah, Mary, Noah, Daniel, etc) is to fulfill His ultimate purpose. For instance, if we know, as per the Book of Revelation that there will be a one-world monetary system, what are the conditions that would cause the nations to embrace such a system? Those economic woes are being experienced today.

Make your life fit into God's plan and stop trying to get Him to embrace yours.

Predestination

Does God have your life planned? Does the word "predestination" make you think that He does? Do you really have choices in your life? Will you end up at God's destination for you regardless of your life choices?

Some people answer these questions with an unequivocal "yes" while others say absolutely "no." The two extremes each have historical significance while they perhaps do not enjoy so much biblical support. The "yes" people would be supporters of John Calvin (1509-1564) – Calvinists - while the "no" advocates would be named for Jacobus Arminius (1560-1609) --Arminians. In fact, both would wear the labels with honor.

In summary, Calvinism centers on the supreme sovereignty of God, predestination, the total depravity of man, unconditional election, limited atonement, irresistible grace, and the perseverance of the saints.

Arminianism emphasizes conditional election based on God's foreknowledge, man's free will through prevenient grace to cooperate with God in salvation, Christ's universal atonement, resistible grace, and salvation that can potentially be lost.
It is not my interest to defend, dissect or even define either of these positions. In fact, the two seemingly opposing positions are

very divisive and remind me of the conflict in the church at Corinth.

1 Corinthians 1

> *[10] Now I plead with you, brethren, by the name of our Lord Jesus Christ, that you all speak the same thing, and that there be no divisions among you, but that you be perfectly joined together in the same mind and in the same judgment. [11] For it has been declared to me concerning you, my brethren, by those of Chloe's household, that there are contentions among you. [12] Now I say this, that each of you says, "I am of Paul," or "I am of Apollos," or "I am of Cephas," or "I am of Christ." [13] Is Christ divided? Was Paul crucified for you? Or were you baptized in the name of Paul?*

The division that the doctrine of "predestination" creates certainly keeps Christians, believers, followers of Jesus from cooperating with each other to reach the vast world of unbelievers. In fact, churches that hold to each extreme spend an inordinate amount of time preaching their extremes, defending their position, and not preaching or performing the great commission. Jesus said that the world would know we are His disciples by our love for one another. We don't love one another, we have denominations instead. The mission suffers because of it.

It is not my interest to name either of the people of a bygone era or even to name people of this era as theologians that I would embrace. I have the Bible and so do you. Do I have to let someone else tell me what it says or can I, with the leading of the Holy Spirit, decide for myself? I have and would certainly seek out the opinions of others in their interpretation of difficult doctrines but I feel no need to credit them with the *discovery* of those doctrines.

Let's get to it.

Predestination certainly *is* a doctrine taught in Scripture. It is clear that God has predetermined *something*. The question is "did God predetermine *everything*?" If not, is there a scope of what God *did* predetermine? The assertion of this chapter is that God has indeed linked together several biblical ideas. *For sure*, prophecy is predestination. Everything prophesied by God will surely come to fruition; otherwise it does not qualify as biblical prophecy. Therefore, the events prophesied are predestined.

Next, I cannot think of any prophecy that does not affect the nation of Israel. It may not be explicitly about Israel, but every aspect of prophecy in some way touches Israel. The Book of Daniel is full of prophecy about the nations, but they all center around Israel. Of course, all of   the Messianic prophecies deal with Israel. The Book of Revelation is all about Israel. The anti-Christ attacks Israel. Even Gentile salvation requires accepting the Messiah of Israel. When "time is no more," life centers around the New Jerusalem. *All prophecy is predestination influencing Israel.*

How do you deal with the word?

> *Romans 8:29-30 tells us, "For those God foreknew he also predestined to be conformed to the likeness of his Son, that he might be the firstborn among many brothers. And those he predestined, he also called; those he called, he also justified; those he justified, he also glorified."*

This verse is loaded with scary words that evoke passion from -"Calvinists."- I however, find something missing in the verse, *salvation.* What it does *not* say is that those He foreknew and predestinated He *saved.* Can it be that God will take those that He saved and conform them to the likeness of his Son? Could it mean that God will not leave us as saved sinners, prone to failure, sullied by this world and accustomed to sin but will, as the "end game," conform us to be like his Son?

Furthermore, there are very few *individuals* mentioned in Scripture whose lives seem to be predetermined. Mary, the mother of Jesus, may have been, but you could make the

37

argument that God could have used any virgin whose heart was for God. Of course Mary met the necessary lineage requirements to birth the Messiah, but so did many other young girls. Clearly Jeremiah was chosen, John the Baptist was chosen, probably Paul was chosen, but there is no teaching that indicates that they could not have refused their assignments. It seems very safe to say that God rarely or never predetermines the life of *any individual* except Jesus. It is most certain to me that God has not predetermined yours. *God's predestination affects nations and events, not individuals.*

Summary:

All prophecy is predestination.

All prophecy affects Israel.

Predestination is NOT for individuals, with very few exceptions.

Predestination predetermines the destination, not the person i.e. "to be conformed to the likeness of His Son" (Romans 8:29), "to the adoption as sons" (Ephesians 1:5), "to obtain an inheritance" (1Peter 1:4).

Why Does God Allow Evil?
(Theodicy)

Theodicy is an attempt to reconcile the existence of an omni-benevolent, omnipotent and omniscient God with evil.

One of the most difficult concerns that have been expressed by believers and unbelievers alike is the existence of evil. Several questions come from the existence of evil concerning its compatibility with God. Since God is considered good, why would He allow evil? If God is powerful why does He not stamp out evil? If God is in charge why does He give evil permission to exist? There is even some logic that says - since evil exists maybe God does not. Let's examine some of these ideas and try to resolve the seeming incompatibility.

Let's start with some logic that has been expressed over the years.

* If God is willing to prevent evil but unable, then He is impotent
* If God is able to prevent evil but not willing, He is evil
* If He is both able and willing then why does evil conspicuously still exist?

This is one way to view the issue. It certainly doesn't cover all possibilities but it is a view. If one *wants* to try to believe that there is no God then this logic is sufficient. If one wants to examine the issue honestly, it will require asking better questions. Consider this atheistic view.

* An omni-benevolent God would not want evil to exist
* An omnipotent God would put down evil
* Since evil exists God does not exist

For the atheist, this is no great problem. Life is a cosmic accident, morality is an arbitrary game by which we order our lives, and meaning is non-existent. As noted atheist and Oxford University professor Richard Dawkins explains, "human life is nothing more than a way for selfish genes to multiply and reproduce." There is no meaning or dignity to humanity.

For the Christian Scientist, the material world and the experience of suffering and death are illusory. In other religions, suffering is part of a great circle of life or recurring incarnations of spirit.
For those of us with a biblical worldview more spiritual logic is required. Consider this triad.

* An omni benevolent God would want to eliminate evil
* An omnipotent God would be able to eliminate evil
* Yet evil still exists

Why? Perhaps:

* God is Omni benevolent and omnipotent

* God created a world that contains evil and had a good reason for doing so

* The world contains evil and evil is consistent with the biblical worldview of God

Or

* An Omni benevolent God would want to eliminate evil

* An omnipotent God would be able to eliminate evil

* God will eliminate evil in the future

Some Christians simply explain suffering as the consequence of personal sins, known or unknown. Some suffering can be directly traced to sin, what we sow, so shall we reap, and multiple millions of persons can testify to this reality. Some persons even suffer innocently by the sinful acts of others.

Jesus rejected this as a blanket explanation for suffering; instructing His disciples in John 9 and Luke 13 that they could not always trace suffering back to sin. We should note that the problem of evil and suffering, the theological issue of theodicy, is customarily divided into evil of two kinds, moral and natural. Both are included in these passages. In Luke 13, the murder of the Galileans is clearly moral evil, a premeditated crime--just like the terrorist acts in New York and Washington. In John 9, a man is blind from birth, and Jesus tells the Twelve that this blindness cannot be traced back to this man's sin, or that of his parents.

Natural evil comes without a moral agent. A tower falls, an earthquake shakes, a tornado destroys, a hurricane ravages, a spider bites, and disease debilitates and kills. The world is filled with wonders mixed with dangers. Gravity can save you or gravity can kill you. Everything winds down and finally comes to dust.

What is evils origin?

* Rebellion of Satan

> *Isaiah 14:12 "How you are fallen from heaven,*
> *O Lucifer, son of the morning!*
> *How you are cut down to the ground,*
> *You who weakened the nations!*
> *13 For you have said in your heart:*
> *'I will ascend into heaven,*
> *I will exalt my throne above the stars of God;*
> *I will also sit on the mount of the congregation*
> *On the farthest sides of the north;*
> *14 I will ascend above the heights of the clouds,*
> *I will be like the Most High.'*

II Cor. 4:3-4 But even if our gospel is veiled, it is veiled to those who are perishing, ⁴ whose minds the god of this age has blinded, who do not believe, lest the light of the gospel of the glory of Christ, who is the image of God, should shine on them.

Eph. 2:2 in which you once walked according to the course of this world, according to the prince of the power of the air, the spirit who now works in the sons of disobedience

I John 5:19 We know that we are of God, and the whole world lies under the sway of the wicked one.

* Choice by man

Romans 5:12 Therefore, just as through one man sin entered the world, and death through sin, and thus death spread to all men, because all sinned—

Psalm 51:5 Behold, I was brought forth in iniquity, And in sin my mother conceived me.

Jer. 17:9 "The heart is deceitful above all things, And desperately wicked; Who can know it?

Matthew. 15:19 For out of the heart proceed evil thoughts, murders, adulteries, fornications, thefts, false witness, blasphemies.

44

Gen. 3:16 To the woman He said:

"I will greatly multiply your sorrow and your conception;
In pain you shall bring forth children;
Your desire shall be for your husband,
And he shall rule over you."

[17] Then to Adam He said, "Because you have heeded the voice of your wife, and have eaten from the tree of which I commanded you, saying, 'You shall not eat of it':

"Cursed is the ground for your sake;
In toil you shall eat of it
All the days of your life.
[18] Both thorns and thistles it shall bring forth for you,
And you shall eat the herb of the field.
[19] In the sweat of your face you shall eat bread
Till you return to the ground,
For out of it you were taken;
For dust you are,
And to dust you shall return."

One question that occurs to me is "Does evil have any value?" If God allows evil, then He must have a good reason for it. Therefore evil must have a good purpose. The new question then becomes, for me, "what good can come from evil?"

Evil is one of Gods' greatest tools.

* God has a morally and spiritually adequate reason for pain

> *Psalm 89:14 Righteousness and justice are the foundation*
> *of Your throne;*
> *Mercy and truth go before Your face.*

> *Isa. 55:8-9 "For My thoughts are not your thoughts,*
> *Nor are your ways My ways," says the LORD.*
> *⁹ "For as the heavens are higher than the earth,*
> *So are My ways higher than your ways,*
> *And My thoughts than your thoughts.*

* God's sovereignty and glory will be displayed by his ultimate victory over evil

> *Heb. 2:14-15 Inasmuch then as the children have*
> *partaken of flesh and blood, He Himself likewise*
> *shared in the same, that through death He might*
> *destroy him who had the power of death, that is,*
> *the devil, ¹⁵ and release those who through fear of*
> *death were all their lifetime subject to bondage.*

* God allows evil and suffering for the resulting greater good

Acts 2:22-23 *"Men of Israel, hear these words: Jesus of Nazareth, a Man attested by God to you by miracles, wonders, and signs which God did through Him in your midst, as you yourselves also know— 23 Him, being delivered by the determined purpose and foreknowledge of God, you have taken by lawless hands, have crucified, and put to death"*

God's possible purposes for evil and suffering

* Draw men to Himself

> *John 12:31 Now is the judgment of this world; now the ruler of this world will be cast out. 32 And I, if I am lifted up from the earth, will draw all peoples to Myself." 33 This He said, signifying by what death He would die.*

God designed life to where we would need him sooner or later. Why would a human desire God if man's life were strictly blissful? If our lives were without "need," we would never *need* God. The human condition, as designed by God, dictates that we will seek God to fill our need for Him.

* Build Christian character

> *And not only that, but we also*
> *Romans.   5:3*

47

glory in tribulations, knowing that tribulation produces perseverance;

Romans. 8:28 And we know that all things work together for good to those who love God, to those who are the called according to His purpose.

Heb 12:5 "My son, do not despise the chastening of the LORD, Nor be discouraged when you are rebuked by Him; ⁶ For whom the LORD loves He chastens, And scourges every son whom He receives." ⁷ If you endure chastening, God deals with you as with sons; for what son is there whom a father does not chasten? ⁸ But if you are without chastening, of which all have become partakers, then you are illegitimate and not sons. ⁹ Furthermore, we have had human fathers who corrected us, and we paid them respect. Shall we not much more readily be in subjection to the Father of spirits and live? ¹⁰ For they indeed for a few days chastened us as seemed best to them, but He for our profit, that we may be partakers of His holiness. ¹¹ Now no chastening seems to be joyful for the present, but painful; nevertheless, afterward it yields the peaceable fruit of righteousness to those who have been trained by it.

It seems clear from the above scripture that part of our growth process, -- physical, spiritual, moral and emotional -- require a struggle, pain. If we lived in zero gravity and never had to lift even ourselves, how much physical strength would we have? If we were given every pleasure that we could experience we would be like some famed celebrities, -- spoiled, self-indulgent pleasure mongers with no apparent moral compass. If we never experienced satanic oppression, how vulnerable would we be to pure deceit?

* Magnify His glory

> Romans 8:37 *Yet in all these things we are more than conquerors through Him who loved us.* [38] *For I am persuaded that neither death nor life, nor angels nor principalities nor powers, nor things present nor things to come,* [39] *nor height nor depth, nor any other created thing, shall be able to separate us from the love of God which is in Christ Jesus our Lord.*

The Moral to the Story

It seems to me that the human concept of "evil" is bad, inconvenient, distasteful, unnecessary, harmful, hurtful, painful, destructive and certainly useless. But God is infinitely smarter than we humans. Perhaps we should let God define "good" instead of letting our concept of "good" define God.

* Evil promotes the greater good.

I know of an old, now deceased, evangelist named Bill Rice. After serving God faithfully for years, Bill and his wife got the wonderful news that they would experience the birth of a new baby. After the birth of their daughter they were stunned to learn that the baby was born deaf. Can you imagine the pain of wondering why God would let this happen to them? They had served God faithfully for years and now He was giving them a less than perfect child.

As time went on and the child grew, they became concerned about their daughters spiritual growth. How could they teach her about deep spiritual matters of God, Jesus and salvation? The couple began to develop a sign language that would express spiritual values. In time the girl would learn, understand and finally become a believer in God, accepting Jesus as her savior.

Since the Rice's succeeded in developing a spiritual sign language they decided to start a retreat for deaf people called the Bill Rice Ranch. After decades of instructive practice, deaf people still attend the Bill Rice Ranch for an annual retreat where thousands upon thousands have accepted Jesus. It surely seems that God could trust these good people with "evil."

I have a friend that has a condition where she can feel no pain in her feet. She lives a very dangerous life because her natural mechanism doesn't work. She has experienced several issues over the years that have done damage to her feet, including braking her feet, without knowing it, resulting in serious damage.

The classic example of good done through evil is salvation being purchased on the cross by an unthinkable evil being perpetuated on Jesus, the crucifixion. The greatest good is yet to be seen, Satan conquered, sin defeated and death finally being ended.

Evil does indeed have value.

Maybe a better question to ask is "Why God allows so much pleasure?" Think about it.

Prophecy

The Bible is full of prophecy. More than 1,000 prophecies have been identified in Scripture with more than 350 of them specifically about the Messiah. Prophecy foretells the future. Perhaps half of all prophecy has already been fulfilled while half is still to be fulfilled.

Features of Prophecy

Through observation, I find that there are several features of prophecy that are notable.

1. Some prophecy is **vague and not interpretable** in advance. It can only be understood after the fact or with much more information. Such vagueness keeps a person from fulfilling the prophecy and claiming Messiahship. A classic example is Gen 3:15, the first mention of Jesus as the Messiah.

> Gen 3:15 "And I will put enmity between you and the woman, and between your seed and her Seed; He shall bruise your head, and you shall bruise His heel."

This statement was made by God in His curse to Satan. It depicts a cosmic struggle between Satan and Jesus, the seed of woman. It mentions injury done to both   the   protagonist   and   the antagonist, Satan and Jesus. It demonstrates a battle of evil and good, with the ultimate victor being good (head vs. heel). We have the benefit of hindsight to be able to interpret this prophecy. Below are just a few of the hundreds of vague prophecies.

* Gen. 3:15, Seed of woman
* Gen. 12:3, Whole world blessed
* Gen. 14:18, Melchezidek
* Gen. 22:8, Substitute sacrifice
* Exodus 12, Passover
* Dan. 9, Seventy weeks of prophecy

2. A large portion of prophecy is **VERY specific**. One purpose of the volume of specificity is to eliminate the possibility of just anyone coming along and arbitrarily fulfilling SOME prophecy and claiming Messiahship. One must fulfill ALL prophecy in order to be deemed the Messiah.

* Gen. 49:10, Messiah comes through Judah
* Exodus 12:46, No bones broken at His death
* II Samuel 7:12-16, Davidic covenant, the linage of Messiah
* Psalm. 16:10, No bodily corruption
* Psalm. 16:9-11, Resurrection of Jesus
* Psalm. 22, Description of Messiah's suffering
* Isaiah 53, Rejection by His own people
* Daniel 12:2-3 Resurrection of mankind

3. Prophecy is **God divulging   His plan** for Israel. It seems to

me that ALL prophecy deals with the nation of Israel or the Messiah of Israel and anyone, whether personal or national, that has an impact on Israel. Even the "church" is a result of accepting the Messiah of Israel. One very often misused verse of Scripture is Jeremiah 29:11.

> *Jer. 29:11 "For I know the thoughts that I think toward you, says the LORD, thoughts of peace and not of evil, to give you a future and a hope."*

I have never heard this verse used in its context. I have only heard it used as a feel good verse to help an individual justify some circumstance that has taken place in his life. The verse is generally used to say that God is in charge and whatever is happening in "my" life is the result of God's wise "plan" for my life. Unfortunately for that line of thinking Jeremiah 29:11 follows Jeremiah 29:10.

> *Jer. 29:10 "For thus says the LORD: After seventy years are completed at Babylon, I will visit you and perform My good word toward you, and cause you to return to this place."*

The context is God speaking to Israel, specifically the southern kingdom, Judah. He is telling them that a piece of their future is to be led captive into Babylon and that they would stay there 70 years before being allowed to return to their land. Shortly after this prophecy was given, Babylon came in and conquered Israel, slaughtering up to 75 percent of the people. The "thoughts" that God apparently had for the nation reaches far into the future. An examination of prophecy divulges the extent of the "plans" that God has for the nation of Israel. The short term plan was to return them nationally to the land. The long term plan culminates in the book of Revelation.

4. Prophecy is generally **corporate**. Prophecy is almost never specific to an individual unless that individual has a direct impact on the nation of Israel. Otherwise, prophecy centers on nations including Israel and others nations that affect Israel. One such person is Cyrus king of Persia. The prophet Jeremiah apparently named Cyrus, before he was born, discussing his role in building a temple in Jerusalem.

> *2 Chronicles 36:22-23 "Now in the first year of **Cyrus** king of Persia, that the word of the LORD by the mouth of Jeremiah might be fulfilled, the LORD stirred up the spirit of **Cyrus** king of Persia, so that he made a proclamation throughout all his kingdom, and also put it in writing, saying, Thus says **Cyrus** king of Persia: All the kingdoms of the earth the LORD God of heaven has given me. And He has commanded me to build Him a house at Jerusalem which is in Judah. Who is among you of all His people? May the LORD his God be with him, and let him go up!"*

5. Prophecy is written too **far   in advance** to be considered a

contemporary happening. Genesis 3:15 was spoken by God several thousand years before Jesus was born and written by Moses 1400 years before Jesus. Psalm 22, a Messianic Psalm, speaks of the crucifixion and was written 1000 years before Christ. Uniquely, this chapter records prophecy about a crucifixion that would not be used but for a brief 300 years of Roman rule during the life and times of Jesus. It was not a method of punishment for 850 years after it was prophesied in Psalm 22.

6. Since prophecy is written in advance and since it must be fulfilled, it can also be called **predestination**. The prophecy given by God creates a predestined event. It may be that this idea can explain the total idea of predestination as a doctrine. Could it be that since all prophecy centers on Israel, then all predestination also centers on Israel? This could relieve some of the tension that is felt on the subject of predestination.

7. Prophecy must be **on time and accurate**. There is no "close enough" for prophecy. If Micah 5:2 predicts that the Messiah will be born in Bethlehem, then He must be born in Bethlehem. If the date of the crucifixion is prophesized to happen before the temple destruction in 70 AD, then Messiah had to die before 70 AD. If prophecy told that Messiah would be born through the linage of David, then He must be born through the linage of David. Close enough is not good enough for biblical prophecy.

Prophecy has several distinct purposes.

1. Prophecy **validates** the existence of God, validates the Bible as God's Word and validates Jesus as the Messiah. In Luke 24 Jesus used the fulfillment of prophecy to explain to those on the journey that He was the Messiah. He asked a very piercing question to the bewildered men as they were trying to process the things that had happened that day. He asked them, "what things?" in verse 19. He was probing to find out what was their opinion of the events. Their opinions were a result of their religion, the teaching of their leaders, and their own prejudice. In verse 25 Jesus called the men "fools" for not paying attention to "all that the prophets have said."

> Luke 24 *"O foolish ones, and slow of heart to believe in all that the prophets have spoken!* [26] *Ought not the Christ to have suffered these things and to enter into His glory?"* [27] *And beginning at Moses and all the Prophets, He expounded to them in all the Scriptures the things concerning Himself."*

The men did not know the prophetic requirements for the Messiah. They thought that *perhaps* He was the one, but how could He be - He had been killed. Jesus explained, through prophecy, that the Messiah would indeed suffer these things. Jesus used the prophecy to validate His Messiahship.

Since prophecy can't be concocted by natural means, it must have come from a power that is supernatural. Since the prophecy is found in the Bible, it must be the supernatural recordings of the supernatural God, who is the author of the supernatural book. It couldn't be any other way and have the prophecy actually be told far in advance. Just like Jesus, Peter used prophecy to validate the Messiahship in Acts 2 on the day of Pentecost. In Acts 7, Stephen used prophecy the same way and Paul did it constantly, while talking to Jews, on his missionary journeys, (Acts 17:1-3). Prophecy is that which validates God, Jesus and the Bible.

2. **Hope** is another great contribution of prophecy. Our world is a very dangerous place in which to live. The world's economy is in shambles. Hatred seems to pervade. War is on every continent. Religious bias seems to run the world's politics. Sexual perversion is turning into the norm. The world seems almost devoid of real ethical leadership. But wait! For those who have a biblical world view, there is hope. We know how it all turns out because of prophecy. Peace is coming with the Prince of Peace. Right will be restored as the evil one is put down. Religion will be brought to naught with its hateful prejudice. We look forward to the "blessed hope" (Titus 2:13).

3. **Holiness** is another byproduct of prophecy.

II Timothy 4:8 "⁸Finally, there is laid up for me the crown of righteousness, which the Lord, the righteous

59

Judge, will give to me on that Day, and not to me only but also to all who have loved His appearing.

This is an interesting link between the heavily prophesied second coming of Jesus and righteousness. Apparently, people who are expecting Jesus to return live more righteous lives. My mother used to have a saying regarding being prepared. She used to say "wear clean underwear." She would jokingly say that I should wear clean underwear in case I got in an auto accident and wound up in a hospital emergency room lying in my underwear. It makes a good point regarding the return of Jesus; don't be caught living in sin. It may be embarrassing. Prophecy about Jesus' return produces holiness.

4. Over and over again in my life I have been **motivated** by the return of Jesus. I have preached about Him for decades. I have introduced several thousand people to Him. I have studied about Him. I have prayed to Him. I have aspired to know Him and love Him. Soon I will get to meet Him face to face. That motivates me to live a productive, holy life, focused on sharing the grace of Jesus with a needy world.

Statistical Certainty

Professor Emeritus of Science at Westmont College, Peter Stoner, has calculated the probability of one man fulfilling the major prophecies made concerning the Messiah. The estimates were worked out by 12 different classes representing some 600 university students.

This mathematical exercise has become a standard for establishing the statistical *likelihood* that Jesus is the Messiah. For instance, each of the prophecies listed below are assessed as to their likelihood. What are the odds that the Messiah would be born in Bethlehem? First assuming that the Messiah would be born in Israel, how many cities or towns were in Israel at the time of the birth of Jesus? There were approximately 1000 towns in Israel at that time. Assuming populations being equal, the probability of the Messiah being born in Bethlehem was 1 to 1000, which is reflected as 1 to 10 to the 3rd power (10^3). You must add your own probability to each prophecy. What do YOU think the probability was for each one? I made up my own, you do the same. Follow the chart below which lists the probabilities of each of the selected prophecies and then adds the "powers" or superscripts to get the overall probability.

Old Testament Verse	Prophecy	Fulfillment	Fulfillment probability
Micah 5:2	Born in Bethlehem	Matthew. 2:1-2	1 to 10^3
Isaiah 40:3	Had a forerunner	Matthew. 3:1-3	1 to 10^4
Isaiah 53:1-6	Rejected	Matthew. 27:21-23	1 to 10^4
Zech. 11:12-13	Betrayed by a friend	Matthew. 26:14-15	1 to 10^3
Zech. 11:12-13	For 30 pieces of silver	Matthew. 26:14-15	1 to 10^5
Zech. 11:13	Friend returns money	Matthew. 27:5-6	1 to 10^6
Psalms 22	Hands, side pierced	Matthew. 27	1 to 10^6
Psalms 22:18	Gamble for garments	Matthew. 27:35	1 to 10^5
		Total of superscripts	1 to 10^{36}

That number looks like this:

1 to 1,000,000,000,000,000,000,000,000,000,000,000.

Those are astronomical odds that one person would fulfill only 8 prophecies. There are actually over 360 prophecies that we could add to the chart. What would that number look like? Staggering!

It is a statistical certainty, proven by prophecy, that Jesus is who He said He is.

Religion

Before we can search for the origin of religion, we must first try to understand the meaning of the word - religion. Already we have a complicated matter. There are many twists to the word and its etymology. A generally accepted definition is derived from two Latin words joined together, *re* (again) + *ligare* (to connect) or "to reconnect," *re-ligare.* The definition therefore denotes an attempt by man to reconnect with God. Since man is trying to reconnect with God, the implication is made that man perceives a "disconnect" with God. Since a disconnect is perceived, we can therefore deduce that religion is man's attempt to reconnect to God, making religion a **man-made** set of ideas, dogmas, doctrines, rituals, beliefs and practices to achieve the desired end, connection with God.

Wikipedia offers a definition that probably fits the worldview of most people in general. I will use Internet definitions throughout this book because they generally project the worldview of most people. These definitions do not reflect my own worldview but create the contrast necessary to demonstrate the purpose of this writing.

> *Religion is the belief in and worship of a god or gods, or a set of beliefs concerning the origin and purpose of the universe. It is often described as communal belief in a supernatural, sacred or divine being. Many religions have*

narratives, symbols, traditions and sacred histories associated with their deity or deities, that are intended to give meaning to life. They tend to derive morality, ethics, religious laws or a preferred lifestyle from their ideas about the cosmos and human nature.

The word religion is sometimes used interchangeably with faith or belief system, but it is more than private belief and has a public aspect. Most religions have organized behaviors, congregations for prayer, priestly hierarchies, holy places and scriptures.

The development of religion has taken different forms in different cultures. Some religions place greater emphasis on belief, some on practice. Some emphasize the subjective experience of the religious individual, some the activities of the community. Some religions are universalistic, intending their claims to be binding on everyone; some are ethnic, intended only for one group. Religion often makes use of meditation, music and art. In many places it has been associated with public institutions such as education and the family and with government and political power.

Several ideas leap out to me from the above narrative:

1. God is implied but seemingly not clearly defined nor is God necessary to have a religion.

2. Multiple religions exist which demonstrate varied opinions of how to reach God.

3. Lifestyle and moral issues can be included that may improve ethnic relational behavior.

4. Cultural differences may dictate the form that a religion takes.

5. Individual beliefs exist which may or may not adhere to the general "religious" beliefs of the group.

6. The definition opens the door to a myriad of religions, perhaps as many as we have people.

7. Each religion may in fact have elements of truth but not necessarily.

8. The above description allows for more than one God. By definition, God cannot have a peer. There can only be one supreme power. To even have subservient gods would require a name change. He could not be called "God."

This author has studied religion and the Bible for more than 50 years and has settled on six basic principles. **First**, religion is man made, with most having a certain amount of truth. **Second**, "truth" is found in the Bible. **Third**, a cosmic struggle exists between God and Satan, good and evil. **Fourth**, many religionists filter the Bible through their beliefs and not the other way around.

Fifth, the Bible is not a book of religion, it is God's Word. **Sixth,** religion is a barrier between man and God.

Did religion start in Genesis 4?

> *Genesis 4 "¹ Now Adam knew Eve his wife, and she conceived and bore Cain, and said, "I have acquired a man from the LORD." ² Then she bore again, this time his brother Abel. Now Abel was a keeper of sheep, but Cain was a tiller of the ground. ³ And in the process of time it came to pass that Cain brought an offering of the fruit of the ground to the LORD. ⁴ Abel also brought of the firstborn of his flock and of their fat. And the LORD respected Abel and his offering, ⁵ but He did not respect Cain and his offering. And Cain was very angry, and his countenance fell."*

The book of Genesis is a book of beginnings. Things recorded there are generally the first occurrences of those events. After Adam and Eve took their giant step away from God (the Fall) in Genesis 3, the next thing that we see in Genesis 4 is Cain and Abel acknowledging God by offering sacrifices. The very first notion of a sacrifice is found in the actions of God just after the fall in Genesis 3:21.

> *"Also for Adam and his wife the LORD God made tunics of skin, and clothed them."*

68

God provided tunics or coats of skin to cover Adam and Eve's newly discovered nakedness. Where did God get this skin? Death had not entered the world until this experience. God must have sacrificed an animal in order to make such a provision. We also know that Abel's method of sacrifice was an act of faith, Hebrews 11:4

> *"By faith Abel offered to God a more excellent sacrifice than Cain..."*

Romans 10:17 tells us how faith is born:

> *"So then faith comes by hearing, and hearing by the word of God."*

We must therefore assume that Cain and Abel had prior instruction regarding making sacrifices.

Abel's sacrifice was accepted by God and Cain's was rejected. A *blood* sacrifice is required by God (more on that later). Cain apparently made up his own way. It may have made sense to him that the sacrifice offered (fruit), being the results of his hard work, was a good thing. God gave him the chance to make it right but Cain's pride was injured and he chose to feed his anger instead of follow God's way. Was this the beginning of religion? It should be noted here that God did not make allowance for Cain's good intentions. Cain's religion did not help him "reconnect" with God.

What was the purpose of the Tower of Babel?

Genesis 11:

> "*1 Now the whole earth had one language and one speech. 2 And it came to pass, as they journeyed from the east, that they found a plain in the land of Shinar, and they dwelt there. 3 Then they said to one another, "Come, let us make bricks and bake them thoroughly." They had brick for stone, and they had asphalt for mortar. 4 And they said, "Come, let us build ourselves a city, and a tower whose top is in the heavens; let us make a name for ourselves, lest we be scattered abroad over the face of the whole earth." 5 But the LORD came down to see the city and the tower which the sons of men had built. 6 And the LORD said, "Indeed the people are one and they all have one language, and this is what they begin to do; now nothing that they propose to do will be withheld from them. 7 Come, let Us go down and there confuse their language, that they may not understand one another's speech." 8 So the LORD scattered them abroad from there over the face of all the earth, and they ceased building the city. 9 Therefore its name is called Babel, because there the LORD confused the language of all the earth; and*

from there the LORD scattered them abroad over the face
of all the earth."

I wonder why they wanted to reach into the heavens. What did they think was up there? It seems that they certainly understood that God was up there. In those early days, first-hand knowledge existed (Adam and Eve) that made them know of God. It would seem that the inhabitants of Babel (later to be called Babylon, which today is in modern Iraq) wanted to feed their own egos and exalt themselves, even to heaven, maybe to become Gods themselves. If you know anything about Satan, it sounds just like him, Isaiah 14:13-14

> *"For you (Satan) have said in your heart:*
> *' I will ascend into heaven, I will exalt my throne above*
> *the stars of God; I will also sit on the mount of the*
> *congregation On the farthest sides of the north; I will*
> *ascend above the heights of the clouds, I will be like the*
> *Most High.'"*

God had other ideas. If their attempts were to reach heaven, their attempts failed. Once again, man-made attempts (religion) to reconnect with God and His domain, failed.

Why did Abraham build an altar?

Genesis 12:

71

", Now the LORD had said to Abram: "Get out of your country, From your family And from your father's house, To a land that I will show you.

, I will make you a great nation; I will bless you And make your name great; And you shall be a blessing.

, I will bless those who bless you, And I will curse him who curses you; And in you all the families of the earth shall be blessed.", So Abram departed as the LORD had spoken to him, and Lot went with him. And Abram was seventy-five years old when he departed from Haran. , Then Abram took Sarai his wife and Lot his brother's son, and all their possessions that they had gathered, and the people whom they had acquired in Haran, and they departed to go to the land of Canaan. So they came to the land of Canaan. , Abram passed through the land to the place of Shechem, as far as the terebinth tree of Moreh.[a] And the Canaanites were then in the land. , Then the LORD appeared to Abram and said, "To your descendants I will give this land." And there he built an altar to the LORD, who had appeared to him."

After the world got corrupted by man's attempts to exalt himself, God chose out a man named Abraham to begin a new race of people with whom He could entrust spiritual truths. He would commission Abraham and his descendants to be the custodians of the truths of God. Religion was to be put down to allow truth to

72

work in the hearts of man. God made promises to Abraham and to his descendants as He empowered them to share this good news of how God wanted to reach man. It will always be God reaching man and not the other way around. My question has to do with the altar mentioned in Genesis 12:7. Did God instruct Abraham to build an altar? Was it a practice that he learned from his forefathers? Perhaps he invented the tradition himself. If so, Abraham or someone else before him instituted an interesting ceremony that would later be endorsed by God as He gave directions for the building of the temple worship directed by Moses. It is a good practice to ask these questions about all religious ceremonies. Did they come from God or man?

What's up with Melchizedek?

Genesis 14:

> "Then Melchizedek king of Salem brought out bread and wine; he was the priest of God Most High. And he blessed him and said: "Blessed be Abram of God Most High, Possessor of heaven and earth; And blessed be God Most High, Who has delivered your enemies into your hand." And he (Abraham) gave him a tithe of all."

A new person was introduced to the world through this exchange. Abraham had just returned from a battle to protect his nephew Lot from the attack of local   powers.   Melchizedek approached Abraham and reminded him who it was that had blessed him and delivered him from the trouble at hand. It was God!

But who is Melchizedek? He is called "king of Salem" and "the priest of God Most High." Suddenly we have a concept being added to our relationship experience with God, a priest. A priest is one who serves as a mediator between men and God. God will later instruct Moses as to the office of a priest, but that will not occur for some 700 years. There was no priesthood. There was no Mosaic law yet. There was no such practice as a mediator. But here we have Melchizedek - a priest. Let's make this clear. God's Word is advocating a priest. In fact this priest is a pre-law, pre-ceremony, pre-view of God's program for reaching man. Later, in the New Testament we have an explanation of this person.

Hebrews 7:

> "*1 For this Melchizedek, king of Salem, priest of the Most High God, who met Abraham returning from the slaughter of the kings and blessed him, 2 to whom also Abraham gave a tenth part of all, first being translated "king of righteousness," and then also king of Salem, meaning "king of peace," 3 without father, without mother, without genealogy, having neither beginning of days nor end of life, but made like the Son of God, remains a priest continually.*"

74

Who is this person who is called King of Peace? Who is this person without father and without mother, without descendants? Who is this King of righteousness? Who has no beginning or end of life, and remains a priest continually? It is the Son of God! In God's program of reaching down to man, He injected His own Son into the world as a Priest, a mediator, the link between Himself and man.

John 14:6

> *Jesus said to him, "I am the way, the truth, and the life. No one comes to the Father except through Me."*

I Timothy 2:5

> *"For there is one God and one Mediator between God and men, the Man Christ Jesus"*

Hebrews 4:14

> *"Seeing then that we have a great High Priest who has passed through the heavens, Jesus the Son of God, let us hold fast our confession. For we do not have a High Priest who cannot sympathize with our weaknesses, but was in all points tempted as we are, yet without sin. Let us therefore come boldly to the throne of grace that we may obtain mercy and find grace to help in time of need."*

I Peter 2:

> *"Christ also suffered for us, leaving us an example, that*
> *you should follow His steps: ꞊ " Who committed no sin,*
> *Nor was deceit found in His mouth"; ꞊ who, when He was*
> *reviled, did not revile in return; when He suffered, He did*
> *not threaten, but committed Himself to Him who judges*
> *righteously; ꞊ who Himself bore our sins in His own body*
> *on the tree, that we, having died to sins, might live for*
> *righteousness—by whose stripes you were healed."*

Now we have two Biblical ideas converging, a sacrifice and a priest. Guess what? Both of them are Jesus. This is **God's** plan. Not **man's** religion.

Abraham got it!

Genesis 14:22

> *"But Abram said to the king of Sodom, "I have raised my*
> *hand to the LORD, God Most High, the Possessor of*
> *heaven and earth...."*

This is a very powerful confession coming from Abraham. He acknowledged the authority and sovereignty of God and recognized that God is owner of all, including himself, Abraham. This is true, simple, unadulterated worship, uncomplicated by the

76

shackles of man-made religion. There were no buildings, no holy places, no rituals, no dogmas, no prohibition lists, no religious garb, no ceremony, no holier than thou people. Just Abraham coming to grips with his cosmic position in the universe, a mere mortal in the presence of God the creator of the universe.

Genesis 15:6

> *"And he (Abraham) believed in the LORD, and He (God) accounted it to him for righteousness."*

No religion here, just simple child-like faith, a relationship between Abraham and God.

Is religion synonymous with spirituality?

Our friends at Wikipedia have a definition of spirituality that is probably in the ballpark of most people.

> ***Spirituality*** *can refer to an ultimate or immaterial reality; an inner path enabling a person to discover the essence of his being; or the "deepest values and meanings by which people live." Spiritual practices, including meditation, prayer and contemplation, are intended to develop an individual's inner life; such practices often lead to an experience of connectedness with a larger reality, yielding a more comprehensive self; with other*

individuals or the human community; with nature or the cosmos; or with the divine realm. Spirituality is often experienced as a source of inspiration or orientation in life. It can encompass belief in immaterial realities or experiences of the immanent or transcendent nature of the world.

This does not sound like the connection that Abraham had with God. Even though many people in the world would embrace the notions of "spirituality," they do not yield to the superiority of God nor attempt to build a relationship with Him. These practices must surely leave a void of peace or fulfillment in a person's life. They are "clouds without water."

It is not in man's best interest to invent ideas that replace the need for God or ignore God's ways for man. Most religionists claim that they alone have found the way to God and all others are wrong, missing the mark. With so many religions in the world claiming exclusivity, it is no wonder that people who seek true spiritual fulfillment are overwhelmed. In fact, if I were Satan, trying to keep people from finding a true relationship with God, I would fill the world with religion.

Repentance

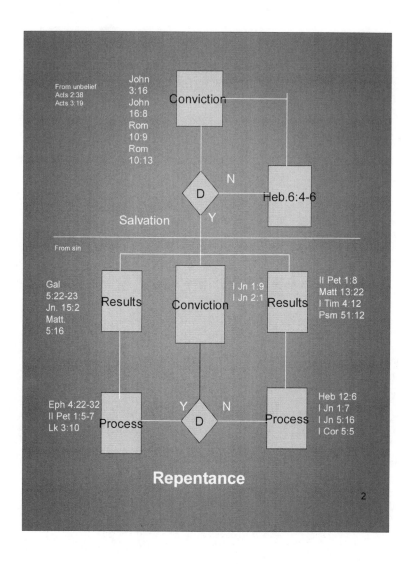

Several years ago, while teaching a Sunday School Class, I was confronted with the word repent from Luke chapter 3. While John the Baptist was preaching and baptizing, he challenged the people to show him the evidence of their repentance. The people asked John the Baptist what they should do to demonstrate their repentance. The reply given was that if they had two coats, they should give one away. Upon reflection it made me analyze the definition of repentance. It became obvious that one cannot give his coat away to gain eternal life. Something else must have been meant by repent.

The word "repent" means to sorrowfully change one's mind about something. One could repent about a crime, a sin, a certain direction of travel, an attitude, an action, a decision or basically anything. The word creates a theological debate that divides many believers and denominational leaders. The greatest issue to me has to do with the role that repentance plays in salvation. By observing Scripture, it is obvious that repentance is a requirement for salvation, but repentance from what, a sin, sins, all sin, an attitude, religion, a direction, a decision, unbelief? It is my assertion that the repentance required for salvation is from unbelief. Anything else would add works to salvation. If I had a besetting sin like lying, would I have to stop lying to be born again? Would it be enough to just be sorry for lying, would that do it? If that were so, then we would have a salvation of works violating Eph. 2:8-9

> "⁸ For by grace you have been saved through faith, and that not of yourselves; it is the gift of God, ⁹ not of works, lest anyone should boast."

Is salvation simply giving away my coat as John the Baptist said in Luke 3? Apparently the idea of repentance needs to be studied a little deeper to solve the matter. The flowchart above and the subsequent discussion may help parse the issue. In order to follow the chart begin at the top left and follow the steps listed in the narrative. The top portion of the chart above the line labeled "salvation" is the process of what happens before a person becomes a believer. The bottom portion describes what happens after a person becomes a believer.

Chart Explanation

The boxes on the chart represent a certain process and the diamonds represent a decision.

Acts 2:38

Acts 3:19

> *Acts 2: "³⁸ Then Peter said to them, "Repent, and let every one of you be baptized in the name of Jesus Christ for the remission of sins; and you shall receive the gift of the Holy Spirit."*
>
> *Acts 3: "¹⁹ Repent therefore and be converted, that your sins may be blotted out, so that times of*

refreshing may come from the presence of the Lord"

Scripture is very plain: The primary ingredient for one to become a believer is "belief."

The two scriptures containing the word repent, Acts 2:38 and Acts 3:19, regarding salvation are very clearly about turning from unbelief to belief. In both cases the issue is raised about the Jews not believing that Jesus was the Messiah and was therefore crucified. The issue would be solved if they indeed changed their minds and hearts about who Jesus was, the Messiah. They were asked to repent from unbelief to belief.

John 3:16
John 16:8
Romans 10:9
Romans 10:13

John 3: "[16] For God so loved the world that He gave His only begotten Son, that whoever believes in Him should not perish but have everlasting life."

John 16: "[8] And when He has come, He will convict the world of sin, and of righteousness, and of judgment:

83

Romans 10: "⁹ that if you confess with your mouth the Lord Jesus and believe in your heart that God has raised Him from the dead, you will be saved."

Romans 10:13 "¹³ For whoever calls on the name of the LORD shall be saved."

The process here is *conviction*. We know that when confronted by the truth of Scripture (John 3:16) and the power of the Holy Spirit (John 16:8), one must make a personal decision as to what he will do with this truth. At the point of decision, one must choose whether to believe or not (Romans 10:9). If one chooses to not open his heart to this truth and not to believe in his heart that Jesus is the Messiah, not accepting Him (Romans 10:13) as his personal savior, he will be then sent through the process of *rejection*.

Hebrews 6:4-6

Hebrews 6:4-6 "⁴ For it is impossible for those who were once enlightened, and have tasted the heavenly gift, and have become partakers of the Holy Spirit, ⁵ and have tasted the good word of God and the powers of the age to come, ⁶ if they fall away, to renew them again to repentance, since they crucify again for themselves the Son of God, and put Him to an open shame."

This describes the very extreme judgment of God upon those who finally reject Jesus as the Messiah. This Scripture was written to the Jews who experienced the influence of Jesus and all that accompanied His presence but cried out in unbelief for His death. They were confronted by the choice and fell away or rejected Him. It is clear from Scripture that even God has His limits. As Noah was building the ark he preached to the people calling for repentance. Even as Noah entered the ark, the people had a choice as to join him or not. Then God closed the door. Once it started to rain, it is my opinion that every person wanted to believe but now it was too late. The door of opportunity was closed. This same idea can be applied to the verses in Hebrews 6 above.

It is not clear how "long suffering" God really is but He will not permit blatant rejection of Jesus indefinitely. At some point the opportunity will be over, a choice cannot be made; the wooing of God will stop.

IF THE PERSON DOES ACCEPT JESUS, then the process is completely different. One becomes born again, born of the spirit, and indwelt by the Spirit of God. Once that happens, life radically changes for that person. With the constant leading, guiding, conviction and prodding of the Holy Spirit sanctification begins. The entire process below the salvation line on the chart is a life long constant experience. One cannot cross back over to the unbelief side. It's permanent.

I John 1:8-10

I John 2:1-2

> *I John 2:1-2 "My little children, these things I write to you, so that you may not sin. And if anyone sins, we have an Advocate with the Father, Jesus Christ the righteous. ² And He Himself is the propitiation for our sins, and not for ours only but also for the whole world."*

> *I John 1:8-10 "If we say that we have no sin, we deceive ourselves, and the truth is not in us. ⁹ If we confess our sins, He is faithful and just to forgive us our sins and to cleanse us from all unrighteousness. ¹⁰ If we say that we have not sinned, we make Him a liar, and His word is not in us."*

These scriptures are written to believers. The issue of sin is at the forefront with Jesus being the remedy for that sin. It is perfectly natural to sin as a believer. It is the goal of sanctification to begin to eliminate the sin in our lives and learn to live holy lives. This life-long process is designed to purge us of sin and produce righteous living. As the Holy Spirit convicts us of sin, we then must make another decision to repent or not to repent. Either way we enter a growth pattern. Growth almost never happens without a trial of some sort or a direct challenge to the sin in our lives.

God expects all believers to grow in the faith. Some of life's struggles are a result of our refusal to grow or repent from our sins.

Hebrews 12:6
I John 1:7
I John 5:16
I Cor. 5:5

Hebrews 12:6 "My son, do not despise the chastening of the LORD, Nor be discouraged when you are rebuked by Him; ⁶For whom the LORD loves He chastens, And scourges every son whom He receives."

I John 1:7 "But if we walk in the light as He is in the light, we have fellowship with one another, and the blood of Jesus Christ His Son cleanses us from all sin."

I John 5:16 "If anyone sees his brother sinning a sin which does not lead to death, he will ask, and He will give him life for those who commit sin not leading to death. There is sin leading to death."

I Cor. 5:5 "deliver such a one to Satan for the destruction of the flesh, that his spirit may be saved in the day of the Lord Jesus."

When convicted by the Holy Spirit about personal sin, if a believer decides NOT to repent, there is a distinct process that God has designed to stimulate the believer to change his mind. He truly loves us too much to let us continue in a life of sin. The above verse in Hebrews 12, is an admonition to "sons" telling us to expect God to reach down into our lives and provide sufficient correction to inspire us to repent. The severity of this correction depends on the strength of our will as we resist the leading of the Holy Spirit and the correction He provides. If a person willfully resists, refusing *ever* to repent, God will go so far as to take that person's life from off the earth. The I Cor. 5 scripture above talks about a person who was a believer but resisted the wooing of God to repent even unto death. His spirit, of course, is saved but the body is taken. Resist if you want to, but expect consequences.

Between the initial conviction of the Holy Spirit and death is a lot of ground. How much is unclear. Somewhere in between is the loss of fellowship with God, (I John 1:7.) Would God withhold His favor from a disobedient child of His? I think so. Anyone who desires the full blessing of God and to be used by Him must participate in the long process of repentance.

II Peter 1:8
Matthew 13:22
I Tim. 4:12
Psalm 51:12

88

II Peter 1:8 "For if these things are yours and abound, you will be neither barren nor unfruitful in the knowledge of our Lord Jesus Christ."

Matthew. 13:22 "Now he who received seed among the thorns is he who hears the word, and the cares of this world and the deceitfulness of riches choke the word, and he becomes unfruitful."

I Tim. 4:12 "...be an example to the believers in word, in conduct, in love, in spirit, in faith, in purity."

Psalm 51:12 "Restore to me the joy of Your salvation, And uphold me by Your generous Spirit."

The unpleasant results of living the unrepentant life include being barren and unfruitful with a life encumbered by the cares of this world. Life can get very complicated. Barrenness and unfruitfulness depict a life that doesn't *count* in the big scheme of things, in the areas that produce lasting, eternal results. Perhaps this life is full of turmoil in relationships. Maybe the lack of peace in the person's life causes him to be hard to live with. Divorces could result. Wayward children may evolve. It may yield a life without a moral compass which can lead to all

89

manner of trouble, excess, abuse, jail, or even suicide.

A believer who lives an unrepentant life will certainly have a lack of positive influence with others. He will *not* be a good example but will instead be a bad example in conduct, spirit, faith and purity. How sad when a person cannot demonstrate to his family and friends, any evidence of his own redemption. They certainly will see nothing desirable to draw them to God. It is little wonder that God will finally withhold the wonderful joy that accompanies salvation. Of course, God will constantly chide a person to live the life of repentance, leading either to fruit or deeper chastisement. The honor of God is at stake as His "children" bring reproach on His name.

IF A PERSON YIELDS TO THE LEADING OF GOD, and chooses to let God clean up his life, another process starts. This process is called sanctification which is the theological term for being set apart for God and His use. *This is the life that God intends* for every new believer. It is the life where God truly blesses an individual and equips the individual for the purposes of God.

Ephesians 4:22-32
II Peter 1:5-7
Luke 3:10

Ephesians 4:22 "that you put **off**, *concerning your former* *conduct, the old man which grows corrupt according to the deceitful lusts, [23] and be renewed in the spirit of your mind, [24] and that you **put on** the new man which was created according to God, in true righteousness and holiness.[25] Therefore, **putting away** lying, "Let each one of you **speak truth** with his neighbor," for we are members of one another. [26] "Be angry, and do not sin": do not let the sun go down on your wrath, [27] nor give place to the devil. [28] Let him who stole **steal no longer**, but rather let him labor, working with his hands what is good, that he may have something to **give him who has need**. [29] Let **no corrupt word** proceed out of your mouth, **but what is good** for necessary edification, that it may impart grace to the hearers. [30] And do not grieve the Holy Spirit of God, by whom you were sealed for the day of redemption. [31] Let all bitterness, wrath, anger, clamor, and evil speaking be **put away** from you, with all malice. [32] And **be kind** to one another, tenderhearted, forgiving one another, even as God in Christ forgave you."*

*II Peter 1:5 "But also for this very reason, giving all diligence, **add to your faith** virtue, to virtue knowledge, [6] to knowledge self-control, to self-control perseverance, to perseverance godliness, [7] to*

godliness brotherly kindness, and to brotherly
kindness love. ⁸ For if these things are yours and
abound, you will be neither barren nor unfruitful
in the knowledge of our Lord Jesus Christ."

Luke 3:10 "¹⁰ So the people asked him, saying, "What shall we
do then?" ¹¹ He answered and said to them, "He
*who has two tunics, let him **give** to him who has*
none; and he who has food, let him do likewise."

*Luke 6:38 "**Give**, and it will be given to you: good measure,*
pressed down, shaken together, and running over
will be put into your bosom. For with the same
measure that you use, it will be measured back to
you."

The process of repentance is described in Ephesians above. The
process includes putting off certain things (sin) but is not
complete until one puts on the opposite of what was dropped; put
off the old man (way) and put on the new man, put off lying and
put on truth, put off stealing and put on giving, etc. That is how
repentance works.

II Peter 1 describes a process of one adding to his faith. The
responsibility of adding is ours. We are the one who does the
adding. We add virtue, knowledge, self-control, perseverance,
godliness, brotherly kindness, and love. It will produce a shift in
thinking, a paradigm shift from self to others. When the

92

people met John the Baptist and wanted his baptism, he asked for proof of their repentance. They asked "what shall we do?" His reply asked for a demonstration of giving, which seems to be the end result of a life of repentance; give of self, time, life, goods, the message of God, whatever it takes to be a blessing to others.

Galatians 5:22-23

John 15:2

Matthew. 5:16

Galatians 5:22 "But the fruit of the Spirit is love, joy, peace, longsuffering, kindness, goodness, faithfulness, 23 gentleness, self-control."

John 15:1 "I am the true vine, and My Father is the vinedresser. 2 Every branch in Me that does not bear fruit He takes away; and every branch that bears fruit He prunes, that it may bear more fruit."

Matthew. 5:14 "You are the light of the world. A city that is set on a hill cannot be hidden. 15 Nor do they light a lamp and put it under a basket, but on a lampstand, and it gives light to all who are in the house. 16 Let your light so shine before men, that they may see your good works and glorify your Father in heaven."

93

The result of the repentant life for a believer is highlighted in the above scripture. Once a person realizes that yielding to the leading of God is the only way to live a productive, peaceful, fruitful, and yes even joyous life, then real life begins. When one yields to the Holy Spirit, the results are love, joy, peace, (inner life features) longsuffering, kindness, goodness, (outer life features) faithfulness, gentleness and self-control (devotional features). This kind of a person would be a joy to be around. They would be a people magnet, a soul magnet, an example to the world that evokes hope and happiness; a fruitful person.

From John 15 it certainly seems that bearing fruit is very high on Jesus' list of changes to affect a person's life. The purging or pruning mentioned follows the physical picture of a fruit tree. When a tree is pruned and the unnecessary limbs are cut off, the nutrients from the tree naturally go into the fruit. A pruned tree bears better fruit. What exactly is pruned from the life of the fruit-bearing believer? Sometimes during the chastising process, as God tries to get our attention or inspire us to repent, He allows things to enter our lives that cause us to turn to Him for help; things that may cause some discomfort or even pain. Pruning may eliminate those things. It may be that if God already has our attention and we are being fruitful, some of life's pains do not come our way. Some of life's distractions are eliminated. In fact it may be that some of the things that end up on our prayer lists are actually God trying to get to us - to turn us.

Finally, a clean, productive, fruitful, godly life will bring glory to God. If a person has grown close to God through the process of sanctification, God will work through him and ultimately bless his life. That does not mean God gives him material goods, but helps the believer have a sense of satisfaction and fulfillment in his life.

Choose repentance. Don't fight against God. Enjoy Him and the life He leads you into. It's why you're here.

Baptism Regeneration

The word baptism is from the Greek word "baptizo" as a transliteration. It has evolved into a wide variety of definitions, but essentially means to immerse. Immerse can be a very general word which can include being immersed in water, pain, an idea, a philosophy or even the Spirit of God. One can be immersed into something that becomes the area of identification for him; i.e. "the student is immersed in his studies."

In fact, in Scripture the word is used in several different ways to indicate a level of involvement into that which one is immersed. In some cases the use of the word baptism is unclear as to the substance of the baptism.

Ephesians 4:5 *"one Lord, one faith, one baptism"*

Is it Spirit or water or faith or Jesus?

I Peter 3:20-21 *"For Christ also suffered once for sins, the just for the unjust, that He might bring us to God, being put to death in the flesh but made alive by the Spirit, [19] by whom also He went and preached to the spirits in prison, [20] who formerly were disobedient, when once the Divine longsuffering waited in the days of Noah, while the ark was being prepared, in which a few, that is, eight souls, were saved through water."*

Did water save Noah or was it the ark?

Romans 6:1-6 *"What shall we say then? Shall we continue in sin that grace may abound? ²Certainly not! How shall we who died to sin live any longer in it? ³Or do you not know that as many of us as were baptized into Christ Jesus were baptized into His death? ⁴Therefore we were buried with Him through baptism into death, that just as Christ was raised from the dead by the glory of the Father, even so we also should walk in newness of life.⁵For if we have been united together in the likeness of His death, certainly we also shall be in the likeness of His resurrection, ⁶knowing this, that our old man was crucified with Him, that the body of sin might be done away with, that we should no longer be slaves of sin.*

Is it water, spirit or into Jesus?

I Cor. 10:2 *"Moreover, brethren, I do not want you to be unaware that all our fathers were under the cloud, all passed through the sea, ²all were baptized into Moses in the cloud and in the sea"*
baptized into Moses?

Water does not mean baptism. In John 3:5-7 the context of the three verses is a contrast between physical and spiritual birth.

> John 3:3 *"Jesus answered and said to him, "Most assuredly, I say to you, unless one is born again, he cannot see the kingdom of God."⁴ Nicodemus said to Him, "How can a man be born when he is old? Can he enter a second time into his mother's womb and be born?"⁵ Jesus answered, "Most assuredly, I say to you, unless one is born of water and the Spirit, he cannot enter the kingdom of God. ⁶ That which is born of the flesh is flesh, and that which is born of the Spirit is spirit. ⁷ Do not marvel that I said to you, 'You must be born again.'"*

The water mentioned there certainly does not say baptism. In context, it is the physical birth. We all know that humans are carried in a sack of water prior to natural birth.

The next few pages contain a description of baptism from a Jewish perspective. Pay particular attention to the word God. Jewish people consider the word itself sacred and will not spell it out. Instead they are likely to write "G_d."

Baptism is Jewish (*Dr. Galen Peterson 2011 American Remnant Mission)*

Not everyone knows the Jewish cultural background of baptism, including most Jewish people. This is especially evident in the way that baptism is commonly perceived today. On the other hand, if we return to the Bible, it's another story.

Who were the first Baptists? They were Jews! This would include Yochanan ben Zechariah, better known as John the Baptist. It would also involve all the Jewish talmidim (disciples) of Yeshua who subsequently baptized new believers. Moreover, it goes all the way back into the Tanach many centuries earlier.

The Biblical Principles of Baptism

Biblical principles are always established first in some manner in Torah. It might be a specific command by G-d that later is brought out in its totality in the life and teachings of Yeshua. Or it might be in a historical event that foreshadows a fulfillment later on. Both of these concepts are evident in the case of baptism.

Exodus—the historical foreshadowing

After the culmination of the story of Passover, the Israelites were released from slavery in Egypt. Exodus 14 tells about how Pharaoh changed his mind and his army pursued after them. When they reached the Red Sea, Moses worked a miracle and parted the waters. The people followed G-d's pillar of fire that was leading them and then we are told:

"But the sons of Israel walked on dry land through the midst of the sea, and the waters were like a wall to them on their right hand and on their left." (Ex. 14:29)

The order of events is very informative to us.

- The people had previously been redeemed by G-d, spared the plague of death and released from slavery.

- Then by faith they passed through a wall of water on either side that was higher than their heads.

- Their emergence on the other side would enable them to become a nation serving G-d and being blessed by Him, when they reached Mt. Sinai a short time later. But at the moment of their deliverance at the sea, they testified in the form of a song, in which they sang: "The L-rd is my strength and song, And He has become my salvation; This is my G-d, and I will praise Him; My father's G-d, and I will extol Him" (Ex. 15:2).

This, then, is the historical context of immersion : G-d does His work of redemption and the people follow Him in obedience. This act is followed by a sign that serves as a witness to the ways of G-d.

Mikveh—the foundation in the Torah

The foundation for all biblical principles, including baptism, is found in the Torah. Within the writings of Moses, it has been determined that G-d gave 613 instructions, commonly called the Law, to the nation of Israel. These principles were distinguished by three distinct categories. There are numerous passages of Scripture that describe the Torah in this way. For example, as Moses was about to give the complete Torah to the people of Israel just before entering the promised Land, he cited each of these categories:

"These are the testimonies (edot) and the statutes (chukim) and the ordinances (mishpatim) which Moses spoke to the sons of Israel, when they came out from Egypt..." (Deut. 4:45)

The characteristics of these three categories can be summed up in this way:

The Categories of Torah Instructions

Ordinances (mishpatim)	Civil ordinances enabling people to exercise justice and to live in harmony, such as laws prohibiting murder, theft, etc.
Testimonies (edot)	Feasts and rituals, (including sacrifices) that bear witness to G-d and His ways.
Statutes (chukim)	Practices that serve to strengthen the bond between G-d and His people through obedience, usually without any explanation why the people should do them. These include the dietary laws, not mixing wool and linen in clothing etc.

The Hebrew word for this last category—chukim—in the singular is chuk. It is derived from a root verb haqaq, which comes into English as the word "hack." It is a picture of hacking or cutting or engraving into an object. Perhaps the best way to think of it is two lovers hacking their initials into a tree somewhere, leaving a permanent mark indicating their relationship. It really has no practical result. It just means marking or signifying something that was important to them.

One of the commandments from the category of statutes (chukim) was the mikveh bath. It involved the way individuals demonstrated their eligibility for full privileges and responsibilities within the community. In the Torah, it is taught that there were a variety of ways that people could become symbolically unclean, such as touching a dead body or a woman during her monthly menstrual cycle. The entire 15th chapter of

Leviticus provides the specific details.

G-d commanded that whenever someone became ritually impure, he or she had to go to the mikveh bath in order to restore one's status in the community. The word mikveh literally meant "a collection or gathering together." Over time it came to be most associated with a collection of water (such as a pond or reservoir).

We also know this about the mikveh—the water had to be "living water" from a spring or river. It had to be running water. The individual was completely immersed under the water (Heb. tevilah). And it had nothing to do with the salvation of the person.

It was all about signifying that you had been given a new life of blessings and responsibilities in the community. In biblical times, it demonstrated through obedience that a person was spiritually clean and eligible for full privileges and service within the nation of Israel.

As a result, the availability of a mikveh has been essential throughout the history of Israel. You can still see an example of an ancient mikveh on top of Masada, the fortress near the Dead Sea where Jewish zealots fled from the Romans and ultimately perished in the late First Century.

Today, many Orthodox synagogues have their own mikvot. The modern version is filled with water to about chest high. Just below the water line is a small hole that enables water to recirculate from a pit on the other side. If there is not a river next door, rainwater is collected and mixed in as the "living water." The Orthodox community will use their local mikveh on a regular basis, according to Torah instructions. The ceremonial immersion of utensils also takes place there. In addition, a Gentile will use the mikveh as part of the formal conversion process.

So there are certainly some common characteristics between the mikveh and baptism:

- Salvation was unrelated to the mikveh bath.

- The person was completely immersed under the water.

- It signified a new or renewed life of blessings and service.

The Baptism of John (Yochanan ben Zechariah)

John was the one prophesied and sent by G-d to herald the coming of Messiah (Mal. 4:5). As someone who had lived his entire life in the culture of Israel, he understood the meaning of the mikveh well. So as he went about preaching G-d's message and people responded by repentance and faith, he confirmed their spiritual transformation with a ceremony based on the mikveh. There are some key parallels between the rituals of the mikveh and John.

- John's baptism did not determine a person's salvation.

   Luke 3:3 tells us that he was calling the people to repent of their sins. John baptized them in the Jordan River as confirmation of that act of faith. We are later told in Acts 19 that when Paul met some of those people who had been baptized by John and had later believed in Yeshua, he had them baptized again. So we are given a clear indication that John's baptism was not the determining factor in the salvation of the people who participated. It was all about believing by faith in Yeshua.

- John completely immersed the individual under the water.

Both Baptizo, the Greek word from which we get baptism, and its Hebrew equivalent tevilah, mean "to dip." The root meaning of baptizo comes from the way in the Ancient Near East that a piece of cloth would be dipped into dye in order to soak up the solution. The process entailed completely covering the cloth, not just sprinkling or pouring dye on it.

- *John's baptism signified new life of blessings and service in the community.*

The reason that the ministry of John was necessary was the spiritual decay of the nation of Israel. No longer were they keeping their hearts pure before G-d. In the ministry of John, he was calling the people back to the purity and sincerity of their biblical heritage. He challenged the people: "Therefore bear fruits in keeping with repentance" (Lk. 3:8). These fruits were blessings and acts of service within their community. He called them to share material goods with others (v. 11), he told tax collectors not to abuse their duty (v. 13) and soldiers not to extort civilians (v. 14). All of these things were manifestations of people living harmoniously by assuming responsibilities by being part of a community. And that was just like the role of the mikveh. Surely his act of baptism in the rushing waters of the Jordan River was a sign of G-d's desire for an active, living relationship with His people.

Baptism in the greater context of Scripture

- *Baptism follows a previous inward change (baptism follows after repentance in Acts 2:37-41; 8:12; 18:8; 19:1-7).*

- *The practice of the early church was by immersion.*

This was the exclusive means of baptism from the beginning. Even in the historical sources cited by Catholicism as justification for sprinkling, the actual instructions say that you may only pour instead of immerse if water is scarce or unavailable (Didache, c. 70 A.D.; Hippolytus, The Apostolic Tradition, 21 [A.D. 215]).

- *Baptism signifies our new life in Messiah by blessings and service in the Church.*

Going beneath the waters of baptism and then coming back up is a symbol of the judgment of dying because of sin, but then being resurrected through the redeeming power of Messiah Yeshua.

> *"Therefore we have been buried with Him through baptism into death, so that as Messiah was raised from the dead through the glory of the Father, so we too might walk in newness of life." (Romans. 6:4)*

Thus we can share in the blessings of worship and fellowship by being part of the body of Messiah, commonly known as the Church. We are able to share in the responsibilities of serving others within the body in a variety of ways. And we can reach out to those who do not believe, bringing things into full circle as we, too, participate in the Great Commission, making disciples of all nations and baptizing them (Mat. 28:19).

Altogether, as we have seen, the same principles are consistently interwoven into different contexts, yet retaining common characteristics, which establish them as being ordained of G-d.

Component	The Exodus	The mikveh	John's Baptism	Biblical/ historical context
Redemption/ salvation	Previously redeemed, spared the plague of Death and released from slavery	Unrelated	Did not determine a person's salvation	Follows a previous inward change
Water	Water higher than their heads	Total immersion	Total immersion Gr. baptizo / Heb. tevilah = "to dip"	Total immersion
Signified	Able to serve G-d and to be blessed by Him	New life of blessings and service in the nation	New life of blessings and service in the community	New life of blessings and service in the Church

A subject like baptism requires a truly biblical understanding of what G-d is saying to us, without being tainted by the distortions of religion that has rejected the Jewish heritage of the church. And Jewish people need to recognize what their own foundations are, without being tainted by the distortions of people who denied that these were ever Jewish practices in the first place.

While we need only enter into the waters of baptism one time, the principles carry forward throughout our lives. We all need to be continually reminded that we are a new creation in Messiah Yeshua when we believe in Him (2 Cor. 5:17), that our sins are forgiven and washed away forever by His shed blood. Baptism further reminds us that because of this new life. we now have a great calling to serve Him, and that we are richly blessed to be part of His believing family.

Dr. Galen Peterson - end quote.

New Testament Baptism

The Baptism of John - Matthew. 3:5-6 (repentance) See the Baptism of John above.

The Baptism of Jesus (Anointing, of prophet and priest)

Jesus was baptized in the Jordan by John the Baptist, and began his ministry after he was consecrated Luke 3: 21.

> *"When all the people were baptized, it came to pass that Jesus also was baptized; and while He prayed, the heaven was opened. [22] And the Holy Spirit descended in bodily form like a dove upon Him, and a voice came from heaven which said, "You are My beloved Son; in You I am well pleased."*

108

Acts 10:38 tells us that He was anointed with the Holy Spirit.

> *"how God anointed Jesus of Nazareth with the Holy Spirit and with power, who went about doing good and healing all who were oppressed by the devil, for God was with Him."*

As a human, He was in submission to God to fulfill all righteousness and was anointed for His ministry like all priests. He received a special anointing of the Holy Spirit for His public mission. Jesus was divinely consecrated for the work of redemption. In Matthew 3:15, Jesus tells us that His baptism was *'to fulfill all righteousness."* The basic action of baptism is identification, so Jesus identified with righteousness in obedience to the Mosaic Law. The Levitical Law required that all priests were to be consecrated when they began their ministry at about 30 years of age.

> *Exodus 40:15 "You shall anoint them, as you anointed their father, that they may minister to Me as priests; for their anointing shall surely be an everlasting **priest**hood throughout their generations."*

He, being a man, needed to be anointed like the prophets of old. He identified with the believing remnant and also with sinners even though he was not one. Remember, he was introduced as the lamb to take away the sins of the world. This was a unique baptism because it had nothing to do with salvation but a submission to the will of God. He identified himself with the preaching of the Kingdom and repentance by John the Baptizer. Jesus identified with righteousness in obedience to the Mosaic Law, to fulfill all righteousness.

The Baptism of Fire (Purifying or judgment)

There are two views on what the baptism of fire means: The first view is there is a judgment coming at the second Coming of Christ when all nonbelievers are taken from the earth. Jesus taught several parables in reference to the end of time when believers and unbelievers will be separated – one parable is the separation of the sheep from the goats, as described in Matthew 25. They will join the unbelievers from all time in hell who are waiting for the Last Judgment (The Great White Throne Judgment in Rev. 20). This occurs at the end of the Millennium when they are resurrected and body and soul are reunited and consigned to the lake of fire. The Bible teaches that this baptism is for unbelievers in judgment.

John the Baptist said in Mt. 3:11

> *Matthew. 3:11 "I baptize you with water for repentance. But after me will come one who is more powerful than I, whose sandals I am not fit to carry. He will baptize you with the Holy Spirit and with fire. His winnowing fork is in his*

110

hand, and he will thoroughly clean out his threshing floor; and gather his wheat into the barn; but he will burn up the chaff with unquenchable fire."

Luke 3:9"And even now the ax is laid to the root of the trees. Therefore every tree which does not bear good fruit is cut down and thrown into the fire."17"His winnowing fan is in His hand, and He will thoroughly clean out His threshing floor, and gather the wheat into His barn; but the chaff He will burn with unquenchable fire."

Fire is often a symbol for judgment throughout the Bible. Examples are the fire which burned the sacrifice on the Hebrew altar, and the fire from God which burned the watered down sacrifices of Elijah and the prophets of Baal.

Fire and brimstone fell on Sodom and Gomorrah. The world will be cleansed by fire as it was by the flood in the end of time.

2 Peter.3:10 "But the day of the Lord will come as a thief in the night, in which the heavens will pass away with a great noise, and the elements will melt with fervent heat; both the earth and the works that are in it will be burned up."

111

Heb. 10:27: "but a certain fearful expectation of judgment, and fiery indignation which will devour the adversaries."

II Thess. 1:8: "In flaming fire taking vengeance on those who do not know God, and on those who do not obey the gospel of our Lord Jesus Christ.

The second view of fire is a purifying affect.

1 Pet 1:7 "that the genuineness of your faith, being much more precious than gold that perishes, though it is <u>tested by fire</u>, may be found to praise, honor, and glory at the revelation of Jesus Christ"

1 Pet 4:12: "Beloved, do not think it strange concerning the <u>fiery trial</u> which is to try you, as though some strange thing happened to you."

1 Cor. 3:13: "Each one's work will become clear; for the Day will declare it, because it will be <u>revealed by fire</u>; and the fire will test each one's work, of what sort it is." (meaning our work on earth will have its test in heaven to see if it accompanies us into eternity.)

The baptism of fire is more likely about the judgment of the lost than fiery trials in a believer's   life.

Matthew 13:24-30 "Another parable He put forth to them, saying: "The kingdom of heaven is like a man who sowed good seed in his field; 25 but while men slept, his enemy came and sowed tares among the wheat and went his way. 26 But when the grain had sprouted and produced a crop, then the tares also appeared. 27 So the servants of the owner came and said to him, 'Sir, did you not sow good seed in your field? How then does it have tares?' 28 He said to them, 'An enemy has done this.' The servants said to him, 'Do you want us then to go and gather them up?' 29 But he said, 'No, lest while you gather up the tares you also uproot the wheat with them. 30 Let both grow together until the harvest, and at the time of harvest I will say to the reapers, "First gather together the tares and bind them in bundles to burn them, but gather the wheat into my barn."

The Baptism of Moses (Submission of the nation of Israel)

1 Cor. 10:1 "Moreover, brethren, I do not want you to be unaware that all our fathers were under the cloud, all passed through the sea, 2 all were baptized into Moses in the cloud and in the sea"

113

Being baptized into Moses signified a commitment to follow the authority of Moses and the cloud that he followed (God's glory). As the nation of Israel discovered that Moses was indeed endorsed by God, they followed both.

The Baptism of Suffering (His Cup, suffering for our sins)

Jesus Christ "drank" the Cup filled with our sins. This was an expression of all the sins of the world put into one cup and poured out on Jesus while He was on the Cross. God the Father judged our sins while they were on His son. The "cup" being spoken of signifies God's wrath towards sin, all sin, the sin of the entire world. Jesus identified with our sin and He bore our sins on the cross being made sin for us.

> II Cor.5:21 *"For He made Him who knew no sin to be sin for us, that we might become the righteousness of God in Him."*
>
> 1 Pet. 2:24 *"who Himself bore our sins in His own body on the tree, that we, having died to sins, might live for righteousness—by whose stripes you were healed.* ²⁵ *For you were like sheep going astray, but have now returned to the Shepherd and Overseer of your souls."*

The disciples asked Jesus if they could be promoted with Him to a position of importance.

Mark 10: 38 "But Jesus said to them, "You do not know what you ask. Are you able to drink the cup that I drink, and be baptized with the baptism that I am baptized with?"

Jesus prayed in the Garden of Gethsemane

Matthew. 26:39 "O My Father, if it is possible, let this cup pass from Me; nevertheless, not as I will, but as You will."

The "cup" being spoken of signifies God's wrath towards sin that would be poured out on him in our place. Jesus indeed was "baptized" with immeasurable suffering.

The Baptism of the Holy Spirit (Immersed Jesus at salvation)

When a person believes - accepts Jesus as Savior, he is placed into the body of Christ by the Spirit and the Spirit is placed in him. He is immersed in Jesus.

1 Cor.12:13. "For by one Spirit we were all baptized into one body—whether Jews or Greeks, whether slaves or free—and have all been made to drink into one Spirit."

Acts 1:5 "For John truly baptized with water; but you shall be baptized with the Holy Spirit not many days from now."

115

Jesus is making a distinction between water and Spirit baptism, just as John did. John's water baptism was an outward display indicating a heart of repentance. The focus was to have a sincere heart willing to turn from sin in view of the coming of Messiah. The Holy Spirit's work would be inward. This is the spiritual work of God to regenerate a believer and put him supernaturally into the body of Christ.

The baptism of the Holy Spirit is a New Testament experience prophesied by the Old Testament prophets. In John 7:39, Jesus, speaking of the Spirit, stated those who believe in Him would receive the Spirit after He was glorified.

> John 7:37 "*37 On the last day, that great day of the feast, Jesus stood and cried out, saying, "If anyone thirsts, let him come to Me and drink. 38 He who believes in Me, as the Scripture has said, out of his heart will flow rivers of living water." 39 But this He spoke concerning the Spirit, whom those believing in Him would receive; for the Holy Spirit was not yet given, because Jesus was not yet glorified.*

This event happened after Jesus ascended to heaven allowing the descent of the Holy Spirit. Its first occurrence was on the day of Pentecost when the Holy Spirit filled the believers. Now, believers are placed "in Christ" at the moment of salvation and they begin a new relationship with God as children of God. The Holy Spirit empowers them for growth and service to Him.

The baptism of the Holy Spirit is for all believers adopted into the family of God. This is how one becomes a part of the body of Christ.

> *1 Cor. 12:13 "For by one Spirit we were all baptized into one body—whether Jews or Greeks, whether slaves or free—and have all been made to drink into one Spirit."*

> *Gal. 3:26-27 "For you are all sons of God through faith in Christ Jesus. [27] For as many of you as were baptized into Christ have put on Christ.*

As we yield to the Spirit of God we become empowered to serve Him.

> *Eph. 5:18 "And do not be drunk with wine, in which is dissipation; but be filled with the Spirit".*

The Baptism of Believers (Identification with Jesus, in water)

At the end of His earthly ministry, Jesus gave His disciples, apostles and subsequent new believers, marching orders for reaching the world with the message of God. It has always been the purpose of God to have   presented to the world the choice of having a relationship with Him. The marching orders came in the form of Scripture, commonly known as the great commission

> *Matthew 28:18-20 "[18] And Jesus came and spoke to them, saying, "All authority has been given to Me in heaven and on earth. [19] Go therefore and make disciples of all the nations, baptizing them in the name of the Father and of the Son and of the Holy Spirit, [20] teaching them to observe all things that I have commanded you; and lo, I am with you always, even to the end of the age." Amen.*

In keeping with the centuries long, well established Jewish practice of demonstrating a change of heart and commitment, Jesus asked for new converts to be baptized, immersed in water. This baptism signifies a commitment to and recognition of the declared authority of Jesus. That's it! No more! The early Jews that submitted to this baptism were pledging their allegiance to Jesus the Messiah.

Over the centuries however, this baptism has become very highly religiously charged. As the "Christian" world took ownership of "Christianity," the definition of baptism took off in all directions. Baptism actually became the *method* of salvation to millions of people at the teaching of the "church." Millions were forced to be baptized during the Crusades in Europe and the Middle East.

Refusal to be baptized would result in death. Adults were forced to watch their children be murdered if they refused to submit to baptism. The practice morphed into the *means* of salvation instead of a testimony *about* salvation. This "evolved" practice then became a dividing point within the ranks of Christianity as denominations were formed that embraced or rejected the definition. Some did, some didn't.

Troublesome Scripture

Not all Scripture is crystal clear for interpretation. This is why one must always compare Scripture with Scripture. Sooner or later, as one studies Scripture, it will all fit together and agree. The unclear will become clear. It is unwise to take unclear Scripture and form a denominational doctrine with it. It is, however, a very common practice. Below are a few of the unclear Scriptures pertaining to baptism. The lack of clarity comes from sentence structure, interpreting Greek words that have two meanings, and a general disagreement with the bulk of other Scripture. The Scripture is not wrong, only the interpretation. If one misinterprets the meaning of Scripture, he no longer has God's Word.

> *Mark 16:16 "He who believes and is baptized will be saved; but he who does not believe will be condemned."*

Those who try to use Mark 16:16 to teach that baptism is necessary for salvation commit a common but serious logical fallacy that is sometimes called the Negative Inference Fallacy. This fallacy can be stated as follows: "If a statement is true, we cannot assume that all negations (or opposites) of that statement are also true." In other words, just because Mark 16:16 says that "he who believes and is baptized will be saved" it does not mean that if one believes, but is not baptized, he will not be saved. That logic can also be used for the Scripture below.

> *Acts 2:38 " Then Peter said to them, "Repent, and let every one of you be baptized in the name of Jesus Christ for the remission of sins; and you shall receive the gift of the Holy Spirit. "*

To the original hearers of these words the meaning was clear. "In the name of Jesus Christ (Messiah)" means to demonstrate submission to *His* authority. They were commonly under the authority of Moses and now they were to recognize the authority of Messiah. The word "for" is translated from the Greek word "eis" which can mean "in order to" or "because of." This is certainly not enough strength to form a doctrine especially in view of the fact that it contradicts other clear scripture.

> *I Peter 3:18 " For Christ also suffered once for sins, the just for the unjust, that He might bring us to God, being put to death in the flesh but*

120

made alive by the Spirit, [19] by whom also He went and preached to the spirits in prison, [20] who formerly were disobedient, when once the Divine longsuffering waited in the days of Noah, while the ark was being prepared, in which a few, that is, eight souls, were saved through water. [21] There is also an antitype which now saves us—baptism (not the removal of the filth of the flesh, but the answer of a good conscience toward God), through the resurrection of Jesus Christ, [22] who has gone into heaven and is at the right hand of God, angels and authorities and powers having been made subject to Him."

Once again this Scripture ends with the idea of submitting to the authority of Jesus. It is hard to imagine using this Scripture as a proof text for baptismal regeneration (salvation through baptism). The water certainly did not save Noah, the ark did. Those who were immersed in the water all perished.

The Heart of the matter about Salvation.

The real issue to me is the subject of salvation - how does it work? It seems obvious to me that salvation has never changed throughout the entire Bible. In fact, the main purpose of the Bible is to give man an understanding of how to be reconciled to God. Therefore every area of the Bible agrees on the subject of salvation and God makes every effort to make it plain to man.

I would cite several Biblical sources to answer the question:

Peter, on the day of Pentecost, preached to the Jews present about the experience of Pentecost. He cited the prophet Joel in the explanation of the events.

> *Acts 2:21 "And it shall come to pass That whoever calls on the name of the LORD Shall be saved.'*

Jesus was very plain in His discussion of salvation. He gave a beautiful picture of what happens in the heart during the process of salvation.

> *Luke 18:10 "Two men went up to the temple to pray, one a Pharisee and the other a tax collector. [11] The Pharisee stood and prayed thus with himself, 'God, I thank You that I am not like other men—extortioners, unjust, adulterers, or even as this tax collector. [12] I fast twice a week; I give tithes of all that I possess.' [13] And the tax collector, standing afar off, would not so much as raise his eyes to heaven, but beat his breast, saying, 'God, be merciful to me a sinner!' [14] I tell you, this man went down to his house justified*

rather than the other; for everyone who exalts himself will be humbled, and he who humbles himself will be exalted."

In John 4, the woman at the well became an obvious believer and immediately began to testify.

In John 3, while talking to Nicodemus, Jesus alluded to an Old Testament example of faith by mentioning Moses and the brazen serpent. God allowed serpents to enter the camp of the complaining Jews as they wandered in the wilderness. The poisonous snakes bit the people and they were under the threat of death. God told Moses to make a serpent of brass and lift it up on a pole. The instructions were given that who ever looked upon the serpent would live. It was certainly a strange event but God was preparing a visual lesson on salvation for us all. The verse below ties it together. Apparently one would not look if he did not believe.

> *"14 And as Moses lifted up the serpent in the wilderness, even so must the Son of Man be lifted up, [15] that whoever believes in Him should not perish but have eternal life."*

Abraham, the benchmark for faith in the entire Bible and held up to us demonstrating personal salvation, was justified by faith.

> *Romans   4:3   "For what says the scripture?*

123

Abraham believed God, and it was counted unto him for righteousness."

Galatians 3:6 "Even as Abraham believed God, and it was accounted to him for righteousness."

James 2:23 "And the scripture was fulfilled which says, Abraham believed God, and it was imputed unto him for righteousness: and he was called the Friend of God."

Hebrews 11 gives us a long list of people, who by faith, were saved from judgment.

These demonstrations from both old and new testaments show the unchanging method of salvation throughout the scripture.

Salvation comes by heart belief, accepting by faith the message of God as He became flesh and satisfied His own righteous judgment on sin by dying in man's place.

I Peter 2:23 "who, when He (Jesus) was reviled, did not revile in return; when He suffered, He did not threaten, but committed Himself to Him who judges righteously; 24 who Himself bore our sins in His own body on the tree, that we, having died to sins, might live for righteousness—by whose stripes   you   were healed."

Below is very clear Scripture. Compare it with the unclear Scripture. An honest heart will easily resolve the issue. A denominational heart will *never* be convinced.

> *John 3:16 "For God so loved the world that He gave His only begotten Son, that whoever believes in Him should not perish but have everlasting life."*

> *John 3:18 "He who believes in Him is not condemned; but he who does not believe is condemned already, because he has not believed in the name of the only begotten Son of God."*

> *John 5:24 "Most assuredly, I say to you, he who hears My word and believes in Him who sent Me has everlasting life, and shall not come into judgment, but has passed from death into life."*

> *John 20:31 "And truly Jesus did many other signs in the presence of His disciples, which are not written in this book; 31 but these are written that you may believe that Jesus is the Christ, the Son of God, and that believing you may have life in His name."*

> *I John 5:13 "These things I have written to you who believe in the name of the Son of God, that*

you may know that you have eternal life, and that you may continue to believe in the name of the Son of God."

Romans 10:9 "that if you confess with your mouth the Lord Jesus and believe in your heart that God has raised Him from the dead, you will be saved. [10] For with the heart one believes unto righteousness, and with the mouth confession is made unto salvation."

The conclusion

Every person that heard the message about baptism in the New Testament fully understood the purpose and the ceremony that was being asked of him. Having been under the authority of Moses for centuries, they were being asked to submit to a new authority, Jesus the Messiah. Once one *believes* in his heart, is born again by the Spirit of God, he is confronted by a new decision; "will I submit to the authority of Jesus?" Every person in the New Testament that became a believer did indeed submit with one exception, the thief on the cross. Unless you are hanging on a cross, it is recommended that you submit and be baptized.

One will never experience the full benefit of being a child of God unless he learns to submit to the will and leading of God.

126

Speaking in Tongues

Introduction

The phenomenon of tongues-speaking is widespread, and it is likely that no issue in Evangelical Christendom has caused as wide a split in its ranks in modern times as has speaking in tongues. That split has proven to be very harmful to the cause of spreading the message of God around the world. If tongues are of God, led by the Holy Spirit, Christianity should be drawn together as was the case in the Books of Acts instead of being torn apart. Where is the disconnect?

All Bible-believing Christians who study the Word of God are in agreement that the "gift" of tongues is present in the inspired Scriptures. In the New Testament, two lists of gifts appear in which the gift of tongues is included. In I Corinthians 12:8-11 "kinds of tongues" and "the interpretation of tongues" are said to be sovereignly bestowed *gifts* of the Holy Spirit. In I Corinthians 12:28-30, "tongues" appears in the list of gifts. What is it? What does it mean? What does "gift" mean? How does it help the cause of Christ?

The Premise

As a missionary in Portugal, I was in desperate need of being able to speak the Portuguese language. That would be a perfect application of "tongues." Why do missionaries require language school when crossing cultures? I personally struggled at every turn to learn the language while others seemed to pick up the language very easily. I longed for language skill. In retrospect, it occurs to me that the gift of tongues may be the *ability to learn other languages easily*. That makes perfect missionary sense to me. As the Gospel was and is spread around the world, fulfilling the Great Commission, the ability to comprehend other languages is certainly required. This is a gift that I do not possess. I am actually to the point where I do not even believe that "spiritual gifts" exist, as normally thought of today. I think that spiritual gifts are given to "every man" (I Cor. 12:3) period. I think that it is God's will that "not any should perish but all come to repentance." The characteristics given by God to "every man" *are from birth* and intended to be used for the glory of God as each person is placed into the Body of Christ. The very first mention of being filled with the Spirit of God in the Bible is found in;

> Exodus 31: *"Then the LORD spoke to Moses, saying: ² "See, I have called by name Bezalel the son of Uri, the son of Hur, of the tribe of Judah. ³ And I have filled him with the Spirit of God, in wisdom, in understanding, in knowledge, and in all manner of workmanship, ⁴ to design artistic works, to work in gold, in silver, in bronze, ⁵ in*

cutting jewels for setting, in carving wood, and to work in all manner of workmanship."

It seems that Bezalel had some "natural" ability, from birth, from God as do we all. It is our choice to use it for God's glory or not. Adolf Hitler had the same gift that Billy Graham had. They could both move a crowd through their skillful use of speech. We know which one used it for God's benefit. I have been a believer and student of the Bible for over 60 years. I have been around the world carrying the Gospel. I have personally led several thousand people to Jesus and have mentored others to do the same. BUT I have never seen nor personally experienced a change in one's skill set once they have accepted Jesus as their personal Savior. It is my assertion that God wills for every person born to be born again into the family of God and that they are gifted accordingly *from birth.*

The Meaning of Speaking in Tongues

The word *glossa* appears in the Greek New Testament not less than fifty times. It is used to refer to the physical organ of the tongue as in James 3:5; once in reference to the flames of fire shaped like tongues (Acts 2:3); at least once in a metaphorical sense when referring to speech as in the statement, "my tongue (speech) was glad (joyous)" (Acts 2:26). It seems that in all of the remaining usages of the word it always means a language.

129

When our Lord predicted supernatural tongues (the only mention of tongues in the four Gospel records), He said, *"And these signs shall follow them that believe; In my name they shall cast out devils; they shall speak with new tongues"* (Mark 16:17). The adjective "new" (Gr. *kainos*) can only mean they were going to speak in languages new to them, that is, languages they had not learned or used until that time

In fulfillment of that prophecy, in Acts 2:4 Luke uses a different adjective when he says, *"they began to speak with other tongues."* The word "other" (Gr. *heteros*) simply means that they spoke in languages different from the normal language they were used to. The context substantiates this. Notice the surprised reaction on the part of the hearers—"And they were all amazed and marveled, saying one to another, Behold, are not all these which speak Galileans? And how hear we every man in our own tongue, wherein we were born?" (Acts 2:7,8). Every man heard them speak in his own language (Acts 2:6). Here the word "language" is the translation of *dialekto* from which our word "dialect" comes. The two words *glossa* (tongue) and *dialektos* (language) are used synonymously, making it obvious that the disciples were speaking in known languages other than the language native to them. In verses 9-11 the languages are then identified. It was a miraculous phenomenon which enabled the disciples to speak in languages which they had never learned.

Here in this Acts passage we have supernatural tongues-speaking in its pure form as God gave it.

But the more serious problems arise in the interpretation of the twenty-one references to tongues in First Corinthians chapters 12-14. There are those who tell us that the tongues in First Corinthians are ecstatic utterances not known in any country on earth. They base their conclusion on the term "unknown" which appears in I Corinthians 14:2, 4, 13, 14, 19, and 27. But the reader of this chapter in God's Word must not fail to observe that the word "unknown" in every place where it appears is in italicized letters, which means that it does not occur in any Greek manuscript but was inserted by translators. The Holy Spirit did not direct Paul to write that the tongue is unknown. In fact, is seems unlikely to me that the discussion in I Corinthians 14 was about *supernatural* tongues. It appears that the Corinthian church was so very carnal that they were trying to show off their "spirituality" that they tried to emulate the events of the day of Pentecost. In I Corinthians 14:26-33 Paul is trying to "regulate" the activity of that body of believers. It is my assertion that the Holy Spirit needs no regulation. No one was regulated in Acts 2. The Holy Spirit was in control. If in fact, the events of the church of Corinth were of God, Paul would not need to impose regulation.

It would be an arbitrary and strange interpretation of Scripture that would make tongues-speaking in the New Testament anything other than known languages. There is no trace of Scriptural evidence that tongues were ever heard by anyone as incoherent, incomprehensible babbling.

Furthermore, in I Corinthians 12 the word "gift" is also not found in any Greek texts. The Apostle Paul writes, "Now concerning spiritual *gifts*, brethren, I would not have you ignorant" (I Corinthians 12: 1). In the Authorized Version (KJV), the word "gifts" is in italicized letters, telling us that it did not appear in any of the Greek manuscripts but was inserted by translators. Paul actually said to the Corinthians, "I don't want you to be ignorant about *pneumatica*" or being spiritual.

It seems obvious that the Corinthians were *anything* but spiritual. I Corinthians is clearly a rebuke from Paul as they tried to show themselves spiritual, yea, even *more* spiritual than others. Before Paul launches into a discussion of being spiritual, he reminds them of how easily they were led astray. He says, "*You know that you were gentiles, carried away unto these dumb idols, even as you were led*" (12:2). In substance he is saying, "Before you tell me about your experience, let me remind you of your lack of spirituality (3:1), and therefore your inability to discern between the Holy Spirit and false spirits" (2:15). They were contentious (1:11), envious (3:3), and full of strife and division (3:3). They were warned about their works being burned up as wood hay and stubble (3:12-13). They seemed to not know that the Spirit of God was within them (3:16). They were judgmental (4:5), puffed up with pride and in need of being rebuked (4:18-21). They did not possess enough spiritual judgment to handle a very immoral issue in the church (5:1-6). The list goes on. It is no wonder that they were called carnal, "babes in Christ" (3:1). Their exercise of the "gifts" were self-induced by fleshly energy, not by the Holy Spirit and were a vain attempt to show *themselves* spiritual; self edification (14:4).

In I Corinthians 12, Paul is trying to tell them that they all fit into the body of Christ, that there is no need for them to try to appear "more" than someone else. In chapter 13, he tries to direct them toward love instead of self edification. He told them with out love "you are nothing" something hard to hear for a person who thinks too highly of himself. By chapter 14, Paul is trying to restore some order in the church and talk them OUT of talking in "tongues." Corinth being a natural trade hub would necessarily have people in the church who were multi-lingual. I can imagine the chaos in a church filled with self edifying people.

The Purpose of Speaking in Tongues

First, to fulfill prophecy and attract the attention of the Jews. Signs were for the Jews rather than for Gentiles. "For the Jews require a sign ... " (I Corinthians 1:22). Repeatedly it was the Jews who asked for a sign. *"Then certain of the Scribes and of the Pharisees answered, saying, Master, we would see a sign from Thee"* (Matthew 12:38). Again, *"The Pharisees also with the Sadducees came, and tempting desired Him that He would shew them a sign from heaven"* (Matthew 16 :1). *"Then answered the Jews and said unto Him, What sign shewest Thou unto us, seeing that Thou doest these things?"* (John 2: 18). *"They said therefore unto Him, What sign shewest Thou then, that we may see and believe Thee? What dost Thou work?"* (John 6:30). Indeed God would give them a sign on the day of Pentecost.

With unmistakable clarity Paul says, *"Wherefore tongues are for a sign, not to them that believe, but to them that believe not ... "* (I Corinthians 14:22). The word "sign" (Gr. *semeion*) in the New Testament is often associated with the conveying of a Divinely-given message to unbelievers. This is the emphasis in John 20:30, 31 where we read, "And many other signs truly did Jesus in the presence of His disciples, which are not written in this book: But these are written, that ye might believe that Jesus is the Christ, the Son of God; and that believing ye might have life through His name." The signs (miracles) were never performed without purpose, but because of the message they communicated.

What *was* the message that was being conveyed in the early verses of Acts chapter 2? The message was that the men upon whom the Spirit landed were the men that would deliver God's Truth. There were three miracles that occurred in those early verses: rushing mighty wind, cloven tongues of fire and men speaking in other languages. The first two were signs to the unbelieving Jews that something supernatural was happening, to which they would show some great interest. The tongues or other languages were to designate WHO God was using to be His mouthpiece. Clearly the men were considered too ignorant to know the languages. God placed the focus on this small group of rag tag messengers. Had they been "learned" men they would not have been considered vessels for the Spirit of God. Peter stood and preached in one language resulting in three thousand accepting Jesus as the Messiah. *There was no language barrier, it was strictly a sign.*

The *only* function of tongues was to impact the unbelieving Jews "for a sign . . . to them that believe not." To try to exercise tongues today would be to violate the purpose for which it was given. The sign was never given for the self-satisfaction or self-glory of the recipients. The men upon whom the sign was bestowed were merely instruments through whom God wanted to communicate His message.

Second, to confirm the Gospel message. It was not merely a *communicating* sign but a *confirmatory* sign as well. When the Apostles used the gift of *tongues* it was because they did not have what you and I have today, the completed Word of God; God's full and final revelation to man. When they went about preaching the Gospel, their message was confirmed by the exercise of the sign gifts. Tongues-speaking vindicated both the message and the messenger. "Truly the signs of an apostle were wrought among you in all patience, in signs, and wonders, and mighty deeds" (II Corinthians 12:12). If one could find an Apostle living today who saw the bodily-resurrected Lord Jesus, he would *not* be exercising the sign gifts because he would have what you and I have, and what Peter, Paul and John did *not* have, the completed written Word of God. Now that we have the Scriptures we do not need miracles to confirm God's message. They spoke with the authority of God as endorsed by supernatural abilities. Today we speak with the authority of God endorsed by the strength of His Word.

A significant New Testament passage which adds to the fact that the sign gifts were given to confirm the Gospel message to the Jews (Hebrews) is Hebrews 2:3,4: "How shall we escape, if we neglect so great salvation; which at the first began to be spoken by the Lord, and was confirmed unto us by them that heard Him; God also bearing them witness, both with signs, and with divers miracles, and gifts of the Holy Ghost according to His own will?"

136

If the Epistle to the Hebrews was written between 65 and 70 A.D. it would be obvious that the people to whom the message was "confirmed" with signs and gifts were that generation immediately following our Lord's death. The Apostles needed the confirmation that the languages afforded. Today we have the complete inspired Word of God.

Mistakes About Speaking in Tongues

Even if supernatural tongues were for today, *which it is not*, there are other issues that would bring the practice into question. Here are a few.

(1) *It is a mistake to assume that speaking in tongues is synonymous with the baptism of the Holy Spirit.* It is unscriptural teaching which says that all who are baptized by the Holy Spirit will speak in tongues. The Scriptures state emphatically that all saved persons have received the baptism by the Holy Spirit. *"For by one Spirit are we all baptized into one body . . . "* (I Corinthians 12:13). All the believers at Corinth received the baptism of the Holy Spirit, however they did not speak in *supernatural* tongues. The question asked in verse 30, *"Do all speak with tongues?"* is so phrased so as to convey the expected answer, "No."

The baptizing work of the Spirit is not an experience in the believer subsequent to salvation. Rather it is that act of the Holy Spirit which joins the believing sinner to the Body of Christ. More emphatically, there is no other means whereby one can become a member of the Church which is Christ's Body. All saved persons have been baptized by the Holy Spirit, but not all saved persons speak in tongues. The baptizing work of the Spirit places the believer in the Body positionally.

Be careful that you do not confuse the baptism of the Spirit with the command to be "filled with the Spirit" (Ephesians 5:18). All believers share equally in this position in Christ and thus share equally in union with Him. There is only one experience of baptism by the Holy Spirit but there can be many experiences of being filled with Spirit. Paul said that not all of the Corinthian Christians spoke in tongues (I Corinthians 14: 5), and yet he stated clearly that all had been baptized with the Holy Spirit (I Corinthians 12:13).

(2) *It is a mistake to assume that speaking in tongues is an evidence of being filled with the Spirit.* All believers are commanded to *"be filled with (controlled by) the Spirit"* (Ephesians 5:18), but nowhere in Scripture are believers commanded to speak in tongues. A Christian can be under the influence and control of the Holy Spirit and certainly not speak in tongues. There are numerous instances when the disciples were

filled with the Spirit but did not speak in tongues. See Acts 4:31 and 13:9-11. To be Spirit-filled is to be Spirit-controlled. Are we to believe that the thousands of mightily used men and women of God who were among the world's best missionaries of Christ's Gospel and Bible teachers were never filled with the Holy Spirit because they never spoke in tongues? Perish the thought!

Can one know if he is filled with the Spirit? Look at one verse in the Bible where the command to be filled with the Spirit is recorded. "And be not drunk with wine, wherein is excess; but be filled with the Spirit; Speaking to yourselves in psalms and hymns and spiritual songs, singing and making melody in your heart to the Lord; Giving thanks always for all things unto God and the Father in the name of our Lord Jesus Christ; Submitting yourselves one to another in the fear of God" (Ephesians 5:18-21). Three things are mentioned as evidence of being Spirit-filled; a joyful heart, a thankful heart and a submissive heart. Nothing is said about speaking in tongues. To sum it up in one word, *Christ likeness* is the manifestation of being filled with the Spirit, and the Scriptures do not tell us that our Lord ever spoke in tongues.

(3) *It is a mistake to assume that speaking in tongues is a fruit of the Spirit.* The fruit of the Spirit results from being filled with the Spirit. The fruit of the Spirit is mentioned in Galatians 5:22, 23 and includes nine characteristics. *"But the fruit of the Spirit is*

love, joy, peace, longsuffering, gentleness, goodness, faith, meekness, temperance." None of the sign-gifts are included in this nine-fold cluster of fruit. The Christian who is filled with the Spirit will manifest the fruit of the Spirit apart from ever having spoken in tongues. As a matter of fact, in Ephesians and Galatians, where the fullness and fruit of the Spirit are discussed, tongues-speaking is not mentioned once. Moreover, in the list of gifts mentioned by Paul, gifts that the ascended Lord bestowed upon His Church, the sign gifts are omitted. *"And He gave some, apostles; and some, prophets; and some, evangelists; and some, pastors and teachers"* (Ephesians 4:11).

All Christians should be filled with the Spirit and all are to exhibit the fruit of the Spirit, but not every Christian has every gift or ability. Spirituality does not depend on speaking in tongues. God's goal for every child of His is to be Spirit-controlled, but that goal does not include speaking in tongues. No Christian need ever feel that he is lacking in spirituality because he has not spoken in tongues. Quality of life is the best evidence of the fullness and fruit of the Holy Spirit. John the Baptizer was filled with the Spirit from his mother's womb (Luke 1:15), yet this Spirit-filled man did no miracles and never spoke in tongues (John 10:41). But he was so Christ-like that people who were looking for the Messiah were led to ask of him, *"Art thou the Christ?"* The key to being filled with the Spirit of God is to yield one's will to the will of God. It will only

140

be accomplished by conquering my *self*-will and offering myself totally to God. If you can get out of the way, God can use you.

(4) ***It is a mistake to assume that speaking in tongues is an evidence of one's faith.*** To the contrary, the persons who seek signs and sign-gifts show their lack of faith. It is a sin for any Christian to seek for signs before he will believe God's Word. As was pointed out earlier in this study, *"tongues are for a sign, not to them that believe, but to them that believe not"* (I Corinthians 14: 22). So you see, the Christians at Corinth were showing that they were weak in faith, and possibly some who identified themselves with the believer had never been saved. The person who seeks any sign, whether it be speaking in tongues or any other sign-gift, is either a babe in Christ or an unbeliever.

Thomas is an illustration of a disciple weak in faith who would not believe without seeing. After our Lord arose from death, He appeared to the disciples.

> John 20:24 *"But Thomas, one of the twelve, called Didymus, was not with them when Jesus came. The other disciples therefore said unto him, We have seen the Lord. But he said unto them, Except I shall see in His hands the print of the nails, and put my finger into the print of the nails, and thrust my hand into His side, I will not believe"*

Thomas was like the Corinthians, weak in faith, demanding to see the sign (miracle) before he would believe.

Eight days later the Lord appeared again.

> John 20:27 *"Then saith He to Thomas, Reach hither thy finger, and behold my hands; and reach hither thy hand, and thrust it into my side: and be not faithless but believing."*

The doubting Thomas needed a sign, so the Lord appeared to him so that he would not continue without faith. And then He said to Thomas,

> John 20:29 *"Thomas, because thou hast seen me, thou hast believed; blessed are they that have not seen, and yet have believed"*

The Christian who will study the Bible and believe what it says will walk by faith, not by sight or sound.

(5) *It is a mistake to seek the gift of speaking in tongues.* It is clear that not all in the church at Corinth spoke in tongues. Why didn't they?

I Cor. 12:4 "Now there are diversities of gifts, but the same Spirit . . . for to one is given by the Spirit the word of wisdom; to another the word of knowledge by the same Spirit; To another faith by the same Spirit; to another the gifts of healing by the same Spirit; To another the working of miracles; to another prophecy, to another discerning of spirits; to another divers kinds of tongues, to another the interpretation of tongues: But all these worketh that one and the selfsame Spirit, dividing to every man severally as He will"

Please note that the gifts were given *"as He (the Holy Spirit) will,"* not as we will, "as it hath pleased Him" (vs. 18), not us. The reason why all the Christians did not have the gift of tongues is because all of the gifts are divinely bestowed. The Spirit divides and distributes to each believer his own gift. Not one of us is capable of choosing his own gift. The Spirit will not give a gift according to our desire and the way we pray. Don't try to tell God which gift He should give to you. We are but members of the Body, and no one member has any right to tell the Head what to do.

It would have been a mistake for the Corinthians to seek the gift of tongues because it is the least of all the gifts. Where the gifts are listed twice in I Corinthians 12, in each instance tongues and their interpretation are placed last (verses 8-11 and 28-30). Note the careful wording in the latter passage: "First . . . secondarily . . . thirdly . . . after that . . . " The least to be desired comes at the bottom of the list, the scale being according to importance and usefulness. The minor place of tongues is further stressed in I Corinthians 14:1, 5, 6, 19. The modern movement of tongues would have you believe that this gift is the only one that really counts and that every Christian ought to have it. The Corinthians erred in overemphasizing the gift of tongues as the most coveted gift of all. To them, tongues was the most prestigious gift, hence its misuse and abuse at Corinth.

Paul charges them with such misuse of the gifts in 12:31. When he writes, *"But covet earnestly the best gifts . . ."* he is not exhorting or commanding them, as the imperative mood might indicate. Rather he is issuing a statement of fact, as is suggested in the indicative. In substance he is saying, "You are selfishly desiring the more spectacular or demonstrative gifts." The word "covet" is not used in a good sense, but in a bad sense, that of self-seeking. "You are not satisfied to be a foot, concealed in a stocking and shoe; you want to be an eye. You want to be seen and heard." And then the Apostle adds,

> I Cor. 12:31 *"Yet show I unto you a more excellent way. Though I speak with the tongues of men and of angels, and have not charity (love), I*

am become as sounding brass, or a tinkling cymbal"

A young man who claimed to have the gift of speaking in tongues said that the biblical basis for his doing so was I Corinthians 14:4, namely, self-edification. But this is both selfish and wrong. Paul did say, *"He that speaks in an unknown tongue edifies himself"* (14:4), but then he added, *"Even so ye, forasmuch as ye are zealous of spiritual gifts, seek that ye may excel to the edifying of the Church"* (14:12). The gifts were given for the edification and profit of the entire Body of Christ, not merely one member. *"The members should have the same care one for another"* (12:25). Self-edification is contrary to the principle of love as taught in Chapter 13, for *"love seeks not her own"* (13:5). The gifts were given for the common good of all (12:7).

(6) ***It is a mistake for a woman to speak in tongues.*** *"Let your women keep silence in the churches: for it is not permitted unto them to speak ..."* (14:34). The prohibition here has a direct relation to the problem with which the Apostle is dealing, namely, speaking in tongues. Earlier in the same Epistle, he told the women how to dress when they prayed or prophesied in the church (11:3-10), therefore he would not forbid them here in Chapter 14 that privilege which is countenanced in Chapter 11. The setting of I Corinthians 14:34 has reference primarily to women speaking in tongues. Now he is not saying that women

145

may not teach or testify or pray, but that they may not speak in tongues. Elsewhere Paul writes, *"But I suffer not a woman to teach, nor to usurp authority over the man, but to be in silence"* (I Timothy 2: 12). The point of this passage is that a woman's ministry must not usurp authority over the man.

If this admonition were heeded today much of the present tongues movement would be eliminated. Women are the worst offenders in the modern confusion of tongues. The word "speak" in 14:34 is the same word used in verse 28, therefore it cannot mean mere "chatter" that would disturb a service in the church. The purpose of this entire section on speaking in tongues is to rebuke the wrong use of the "gift." Verses 27-33 give instruction for *men* in the matter of speaking in tongues. *"If any man speak in an unknown tongue . . ."* (14:27); verses 34-36 are directed to "women" exercising the "gift" of tongues; seeking self edification. And if any women wanted to take issue with Paul, he would ask them one question, *"Which book in all the inspired Scriptures was written as the result of the Holy Spirit revealing to the woman?"* (Verse 36). It is a mistake for a woman to speak in tongues.

(7) ***It is a mistake to assume that the sign-gifts are given to believers today.*** Now I am not arbitrarily closing the door on miracles. God does intervene in supernatural ways performing miracles when and wherever He pleases to do so. The subject be-

146

fore us now is whether or not the Bible teaches that certain gifts were temporarily given. The evidence of God's Word must be the final source of authority. I am stressing this because there are many persons who are not students of the Bible, therefore their only source of knowledge and understanding is subjective, namely, reason or experience. Whatever appeals to their reason, or whatever experiences they have had, settles a matter for them once and for all time.

It is not uncommon to hear someone say something like this: "I cannot believe in Hell because I cannot conceive a loving God sending anyone to such a place of torment." Such persons might listen to clear and sound expositions on the biblical doctrine of Hell, and yet they will reject what the Bible teaches because of their inner feelings and rationale. And so their rationalization becomes their final authority.

Now I am not suggesting that there is no validity in experience or reason. I am quite sure that there are times when one's reason and experience are correct and therefore reliable. But neither reason nor experience can be accepted as final authority. Someone will argue: "I have had the experience of speaking in tongues; I find this experience in the New Testament; therefore my experience is true." Any trained Christian philosopher will tell you that such an argument is not valid because it makes experience the basis of truth, so if one does not experience all of the experiences he does not have all of the truth. True Christian philosophy moves from truth to experience, therefore any valid Christian experience must be determined by the right interpretation of Holy Scripture. Experience, which is related to our emotions, can be deceptive, but a correct interpretation of God's Word can never deceive. We come now to the question, "Is the gift of tongues a part of God's program for the Church today?" If it is, then we would be wrong if we closed our minds to it. If it is not, then we are wrong if we insist upon the exercise of tongues-speaking.

Love is Better!

Let us turn to I Corinthians 13. Now keep in mind the fact that the subject in Chapters 12-14 is being spiritual, with the main emphasis on tongues, because "tongues" was what was being abused. Chapter 12 concludes with "tongues" (12:30) and Chapter 13, begins with "tongues" (13:1). Obviously from the behavior of the Corinthians they were lacking in the fruit of the Spirit, namely, love. And so in Chapter 13 the Apostle dwells upon the essential ingredient of love which supersedes the gifts, and without which the Christian is nothing at all.

Among the Corinthians there were quarreling and division, but the needed fruit of the Spirit, love, was missing. Paul writes, "Though I speak with the tongues of men and of angels, and have not charity (or love), I am become as sounding brass, or a tinkling cymbal" (13 :1). In Corinth the tongues-speaking amounted to so much noise because carnality had invaded their practice. Even today there is a kind of spiritual prestige associated with tongues-speaking. For a Christian to show off anything that God has given manifests pride that is lacking in love. Where love is lacking, the exercise of any gift is worthless.

If Christians would take seriously, within context, all of the teaching about tongues in I Corinthians, they could not fail to see that tongues-speaking does not exist. Paul writes, *"Charity (love) never faileth: but whether there be prophecies, they shall fail; whether there be tongues, they shall cease; whether there be knowledge, it shall vanish away"* (13:8). There will always be the need for love, therefore love will never drop off. But when the canon of Scripture is made "perfect" (or complete), there will be no further revelation from God, neither in predictive prophecy nor in divinely revealed knowledge other than prophecy. The gifts of "prophecy" and "knowledge" will be entirely unnecessary with the completion of the Scriptures.

Paul acknowledged the incomplete nature of the Scriptures in his day when he said, "For we know in part, and we prophecy in part" (13:9), or more literally from the Greek, *"For in part we are knowing, and in part we are prophesying."* Then he adds, *"But when that which is perfect is come, then that which is in part shall be done away"* (13:10). The word *perfect* is in the

149

neuter gender, and therefore refers to the perfect (finished or completed) Word of God. If the word *perfect* referred to Christ it would be in the masculine gender. The sign gifts were "done away" (rendered inoperative) with the completion of the New Testament and the death of the Apostles.

Now what about tongues? *"Whether there be tongues, they shall cease"* (13:8). Tongues shall cease (Gr. pauo), that is, they shall come to a complete halt. Who needs tongues? Only the untaught, carnal babes in Christ, for Paul added, *"When I was a child, I spake as a child ... but when I became a man, I put away childish things"* (13:11). The word "spake" in context can only refer to speaking in tongues. Paul himself came to the place of Christian maturity, through God's revelation to him, where tongues were no longer necessary. And so in the same tongues context he admonishes the Corinthians, "Brethren, be not children in understanding ... but in understanding be men" (14:20). Experientially, tongues cease when the Christian matures on a diet of the meat of God's Word.

How then can we account for the wide-spread practice of speaking in tongues? I do not have all of the answers to this question, but I will make three suggestions for your prayerful consideration.

First, speaking in tongues can be self-induced. *Second*, speaking in tongues can be group-induced. *Third*, speaking in tongues can be satanically-induced. It certainly is not God induced.

Since the creation of man Satan's insidious master-plan has been to put a veil between God's children and God's inerrant Word. It began in the Garden of Eden when the Devil asked Mother Eve, "Yea, hath God said . . . ?" (Genesis 3: 1), thereby raising doubt as to the authority and authenticity of what God has said. We know that this enemy has stepped up the pace of his strategy. One of the characteristics of the anti-Christ is that he will use "biblical" signs to deceive men into believing that he is the Christ. II Thess. 2:9 tells us "The coming of the *lawless one* is according to the working of Satan, with all power, signs, and lying wonders." The signs and lying wonders must seemingly be Biblical or else who would believe them. Beware of signs and lying wonders.

HISTORY DECRIES THE PRESENT MOVEMENT

Several decades ago, a distinguished American educator, Dr. George B. Cutten of Colgate University, took a close look at any historical instances of speaking in tongues. After thorough research, it was Cutten's conclusion that in the ancient church at least, the church of the fathers, there was not one well-attested instance of any person who exercised speaking in tongues or even

151

pretended to exercise it. In the **second century** Irenaeus wrote that he had heard that there were some who spoke in all sorts of languages which seemed to be an ability to learn and use languages cross-culturally.

It is worth noting that his contemporary, Justin Martyr, also "heard" of prophetic gifts, but he does not specifically mention tongues. Origen in the **next century** claimed that there were some prophets in his day who spoke prophetic utterances rather than the use of other languages. It was Chrysostom of the **fourth century** who attested to the fact that speaking in languages had stopped altogether even among fringe groups.

The **Middle Ages** constituted a long millennium of darkness and yet the light shone largely through those of the line of descent or the trail of testimony otherwise known as "the remnant." The **Reformation** era was marked by a tremendous outburst of vitality in grasping again the great, Scriptural doctrines of sin, justification, the inspiration of the Word, and the true nature of the church. Actually, speaking in tongues played no part in the Reformation movement. Thousands of earnest Christians all over Europe sought to re-establish earnestly and completely New Testament doctrine and holy living. Scriptures were searched diligently by some of the finest minds that the church has known. Excellent treatises were produced, outstanding creedal statements were formulated, and men set themselves to discover again the full teaching of the New Testament. Not one of these even intimated that the doctrine of speaking in tongues had a part in the continuing stream of God's work or in the present-day activity in which the Holy Spirit directs.

Speaking in tongues is indeed a new thing in American Christianity. In the founding days of our country our Pilgrim Fathers, Puritan leaders, Baptist preachers, Presbyterian divines, and Methodist laymen did not at all indulge in this practice. They indeed did have times of great emotional conviction and were moved to show their convictions through their fervency and feelings. However, they did not feel led of the Spirit of God to demonstrate this through miracles, healing, gifts, speaking in tongues, or in interpretation of tongues. Even in the strenuous days of the Great Awakening and the days of spiritual heat of the frontier revivals these things did not occur. Thousands were greatly moved, convicted of their sin but they made no expression of any ethereal languages. The Holy Spirit was powerfully experienced in the lives of men but without any demonstration of tongues.

Actually, Pentecostalism itself began in the nineteenth century. One of the main proponents of tongues was Joseph Smith of Mormon fame. It will be remembered by the students of Mormonism that Joseph Smith believed in the gift of tongues along with visions, revelations, etc. To him, tongues would

153

accompany the reception of the Holy Spirit and would open the door for visionary understandings and revelations. After all, this is the way the Book of Mormon had come to him. Frankly he needed this special gift to exist just to justify his receiving his religious book.

Pentecostalism cannot be dated much earlier than 1900. Some did live before that time who claimed "Pentecostal Holiness," and "Pentecostal Fullness," while others engaged in "Tarrying and Speaking" meetings. However, very few of these things occurred before 1900. A Rev. David Awrey of Delaware, Ohio, claimed he had the Spirit of fullness in 1890. In 1897 a Holiness convention was held in New England composed of "gift people." In the year 1900 Charles F. Parham opened the Bethel Bible School in Topeka, Kansas, and this school held that the signs of tongues and healing should be normal for the church. Then W. J. Seymour became greatly enamored with the message of Pentecost and started the Azusa Street Assembly in Los Angeles in 1906. This may be as good a date as any for the birthday of the modern Pentecostal movement. One of the members of this group, G. B. Cashwell, left Los Angeles and went to North Carolina, and in 1908 preached at the annual meeting of the Church of God in Cleveland, Tennessee, where the leader, A. J. Tomlinson, got the "baptism" and the Church of God became Pentecostal.

Conclusion

Pentecostal churches are not Pentecostal. In Pentecostal churches, is there a rushing mighty wind, are there cloven tongues of fire, and is there a demonstration of speaking in known languages to those present? If not then there is no other precedent anywhere in the Bible for what happens in Pentecostal churches. Pentecost was the brilliant move of God to re-gather the Jews of the Diaspora (dispersion) from the countries in the known world, convince them that Jesus is the Messiah, fill them with the Holy Spirit and send them back to their own countries. It would jump-start the Gospel message to the world. Don't miss the point.

Storehouse Tithing

Storehouse tithing asserts that today's Christian church mirrors the Old Testament temple where "tithes" were brought for the support of the temple and the ministers serving therein. It also asserts that the local church bears the responsibility for evangelizing the world through winning, training, sending and financing the global effort.

I was brought up in a Baptist church that practiced storehouse tithing. Years later, I served as an associate pastor in a church that preached and practiced storehouse tithing. After that, I actually pastored two churches where I preached and practiced storehouse tithing. I have, however, always felt a little uncomfortable with the struggle of making storehouse tithing fit within New Testament theology. Of necessity I felt that storehouse tithing was required to support the work of God and that it would be a mistake to even entertain the idea that there was another way.

My attempt to justify it included: Tithing happened before the law (Gen. 14:18-19), was incorporated into the law (Numbers 17-18), with-holding it was punishable (Malachi 3:10), Jesus endorsed it after the law (Matthew. 23:23). In my heart I felt a lack of New Testament inclusion, which I ultimately treated as immaterial. After all, the work of God must go forth.

For the last couple of decades I have been involved in what today would be labeled para-church organizations. This means that the ministry operates outside of the authority of the local church. Our mission of course conformed to the Great Commission but was financed without the benefit of storehouse tithing. Even though it was always a struggle to finance the ministry, I resisted any notion that "church" money should be redirected to "other" ministries.

For years I have known missionaries who would go from church to church "begging" for support in order to perform at the global level in reaching the world for Jesus. Most often the missionaries would devote two to three years of "deputation" in order to raise the support needed to enter other countries. In today's global economy, most countries will not allow a missionary to enter their country if they are not supported sufficiently as to not be a strain on that country's economy. I have seen many, many missionaries abandon their quest to raise support after several frustrating years on the circuit.

It was with fear and trembling that I entered this study of storehouse tithing. How difficult it is to open one's mind to entertain *other* ideas. I tried to lay aside all previous ideas and look afresh at the subject.

Any student of the Bible knows that he must pay attention to the very first time something is mentioned in the Bible. In the case of tithing, it first occurs in Genesis 14.

> *"18 Then Melchizedek king of Salem brought out bread and wine; he was the priest of God Most High. 19 And he blessed him and said: "Blessed be Abram of God Most High, Possessor of heaven and earth; 20 And blessed be God Most High, Who has delivered your enemies into your hand." And he gave him a tithe of all."*

Abraham had just returned from a battle in which he helped deliver his nephew Lot from some unsavory kings in the Promised Land. He encountered a priest as noted above. Not much is said about this encounter except that he fed Abraham and pronounced a blessing on him, perhaps drawing Abraham's attention on the fact that his victory came because of God. Consequently, Abraham, for a reason which is unstated, gave the priest a tithe of all that he had. This priest is a bit of a mystery because there was not heretofore any mention of a priest. In fact, the priesthood would not be established until 700 years later under Moses. Later in Psalms 110:4 he would be mentioned again in a prophetic way pointing to Jesus.

> *"The LORD has sworn And will not relent,*
> *"You are a priest forever According to the order*
> *of Melchizedek."*

When the writer of Hebrews was trying to convince the Jews that Jesus was the Messiah of the Old Testament, he told them, in my opinion, that Melchizedek was actually Jesus showing up in the Old Testament. The clinching phrase supporting that thought for me is found in Hebrews 7:1-3 the last 4 words: "remains a priest continually."

> *"For this Melchizedek, king of Salem, priest of the Most High God, who met Abraham returning from the slaughter of the kings and blessed him, ² to whom also Abraham gave a tenth part of all, first being translated "king of righteousness," and then also king of Salem, meaning "king of peace," ³ without father, without mother, without genealogy, having neither beginning of days nor end of life, but made like the Son of God, **remains a priest continually**."*

It was Jesus and He is STILL the high priest. Since Jesus was declared to be the High Priest 3 chapters before this in Hebrews 4:14 and He appears before the priesthood was established, it stands to reason that Jesus is and has always been the priest of God, interceding for mankind.

Heb. 4:14 "Seeing then that we have a great High Priest who has passed through the heavens, Jesus the Son of God .... "

Melchizedek (Jesus) did only two things as recorded in Gen. 14. He received tithes and blessed Abraham. This is the pattern presented for us to which we should pay close attention. Bear in mind that tithing was not a part of the law yet because the law did not even exist. But it seemed right to Abraham to give tithes to this priest who represented the God who owned it all.

A Purpose Established

Under Moses, God gave the law to the Children of Israel. Included in the law was the idea of tithing. In fact, the word tithe was defined as a tenth. The tithe was declared by God to be His, Leviticus 27:30.

> *"And all the tithe of the land, whether of the seed of the land or of the fruit of the tree, is the LORD's. It is holy to the LORD."*

This chapter describes the natural living of the Israelites. The fruit, animals and product of their labors is mentioned in this chapter. The clear purpose of the tithe was to be given to the Levites, the tribe appointed to be the ministers of God to the people of Israel; Numbers 18:21-24

21 "Behold, I have given the children of Levi all the tithes in Israel as an inheritance in return for the work which they perform, the work of the tabernacle of meeting. 22 Hereafter the children of Israel shall not come near the tabernacle of meeting, lest they bear sin and die. 23 But the Levites shall perform the work of the tabernacle of meeting, and they shall bear their iniquity; it shall be a statute forever, throughout your generations, that among the children of Israel they shall have no inheritance. 24 For the tithes of the children of Israel, which they offer up as a heave offering to the LORD, I have given to the Levites as an inheritance; therefore I have said to them, 'Among the children of Israel they shall have no inheritance.'"

Apparently God did not want the ministers to have to worry or busy themselves with work other than ministering. What a blessing that their entire focus could be on serving God without distraction. A famous man (Jesus) once said, Matthew. 6:24 "No man can serve two masters."

Withholding this property of God, the tithe, became a major issue with God. He used the prophet Malachi to condemn the practice of misusing God's substance and curse the people in Malachi 3:8-9.

162

> *"Will a man rob God? Yet you have robbed Me!*
> *But you say, 'In what way have we robbed You?'*
> *In tithes and offerings. ⁹ You are cursed with a*
> *curse, For you have robbed Me, Even this whole*
> *nation."*

It has been asserted that since stealing is a part of the moral law that this theft is a moral issue and not a ceremonial issue. It wasn't a part of the ceremonial law but the moral law. It does make sense. Malachi's condemnation is actually leveled at the Levites and not the nation as a whole. It would be the priests that had failed in their spiritual leadership of Israel.

New Testament Fulfillments

The Old Testament demonstrates for us New Testament practices. Many very significant examples are given to us to show us how our faith should be practiced. The Old Testament pictures are for our admonition and find their fulfillment in the New Testament. It is clear that God gives pictures, stories, examples, rituals and more for our instruction, I Tim. 3:16-17.

> *"All Scripture is given by inspiration of God,*
> *and is profitable for doctrine, for reproof, for*
> *correction, for instruction in righteousness, ¹⁷ that*
> *the man of God may be complete, thoroughly*
> *equipped for every good work."*

163

It seems apparent that God has a mission and that He wants us equipped to perform it. One classic Scripture that hones in on the purpose of the Old Testament is II Cor. 1-11.

"Moreover, brethren, I do not want you to be unaware that all our fathers were under the cloud, all passed through the sea, ² all were baptized into Moses in the cloud and in the sea, ³ all ate the same spiritual food, ⁴ and all drank the same spiritual drink. For they drank of that spiritual Rock that followed them, and that Rock was Christ. ⁵ But with most of them God was not well pleased, for their bodies were scattered in the wilderness. ⁶ Now these things became our examples, to the intent that we should not lust after evil things as they also lusted. ⁷ And do not become idolaters as were some of them. As it is written, "The people sat down to eat and drink, and rose up to play." ⁸ Nor let us commit sexual immorality, as some of them did, and in one day twenty-three thousand fell; ⁹ nor let us tempt Christ, as some of them also tempted, and were destroyed by serpents; ¹⁰ nor complain, as some of them also complained, and were destroyed by the destroyer. ¹¹ **Now all these things happened to them as examples, and they were written for our admonition, upon whom the ends of the**

ages have come."

Other examples which find there fulfillment, or take on a new form, in the New Testament includes:

Passover, Exodus 12 – Jesus is the Passover, I Cor. 5:7
Priesthood, Exodus 28 – Jesus is our priest, Heb. 4:14
Sacrifice, Exodus 20:24 – Jesus is our sacrifice, Heb. 10:12
Circumcision, John 7:22 – circumcise the heart, Romans. 2:29

Others would include the feast days, pillars of fire and cloud, Passover feast which became communion and even baptism (see baptism in this book). It stands to reason to me that God's tithe, which supports His ministers in the Old Testament, would also support His ministers in the New Testament, except with a global view. In fact similar language is used in both testaments describing them as "gifts" to the world.

> *Numbers 18:6 "Behold, I Myself have taken your brethren the Levites from among the children of Israel; they are a **gift** to you, given by the LORD, to do the work of the tabernacle of meeting."*

> Eph. 4:11 *"Therefore He says: "When He ascended on high, He led captivity captive, And gave **gifts** to men." …………… And He Himself gave some to be apostles, some prophets, some*

165

evangelists, and some pastors and teachers, 12 for the equipping of the saints for the work of ministry, for the edifying of the body of Christ"

When Melchizedek received Abraham's tithe on earth, they were also received by God in heaven, that is true because Jesus is Melchizedek. Later the tithes would be given to the Levites, God's ministers. The writer of Hebrews affirms this matter in the New Testament. When tithes are given on earth Jesus receives them in Heaven.

> *Hebrews 7:4-8 "4 Now consider how great this man was, to whom even the patriarch Abraham gave a tenth of the spoils. 5 And indeed those who are of the sons of Levi, who receive the priesthood, have a commandment to receive tithes from the people according to the law, that is, from their brethren, though they have come from the loins of Abraham; 6 but he whose genealogy is not derived from them received tithes from Abraham and blessed him who had the promises. 7 Now beyond all contradiction the lesser is blessed by the better. 8 Here mortal men receive tithes, but there he receives them, of whom it is witnessed that he lives.*

In verse 8 above, the writer said, "receive them", not

"received them" because he knew that God's pattern of tithing was still in effect. His words could be translated like this: "On the one hand, men (mortals) **are receiving** tithes here, but there, **He is receiving them.**" There is no hint in this New Testament author's words that he viewed tithing as a thing of the past. Quite the contrary, the present tense verb he used indicates just the opposite, that tithing is an ongoing activity in the kingdom of God. The indication is that God's system of tithes and offerings is still in effect because Jesus is "a priest **forever**, after the order of Melchizedek."

Further New Testament scripture, affirming the support of God's ministers, is found in I Cor. 9:9 connecting the Law of Moses in the Old Testament practice to the New Testament need to maintain ministers as they perform the new global initiative.

> *⁹ For it is written in the law of Moses, "You shall not muzzle an ox while it treads out the grain." Is it oxen God is concerned about? ¹⁰ Or does He say it altogether for our sakes? For our sakes, no doubt, this is written, that he who plows should plow in hope, and he who threshes in hope should be partaker of his hope. ¹¹ If we have sown spiritual things for you, is it a great thing if we reap your material things? ¹² If others are*

partakers of this right over you, are we not even more?

Jesus taught us how to prioritize our own thinking regarding money in Matthew. 6:19-20

> *"Do not lay up for yourselves treasures on earth, where moth and rust destroy and where thieves break in and steal; ²⁰ but lay up for yourselves treasures in heaven, where neither moth nor rust destroys and where thieves do not break in and steal."*

This can only be done by giving "treasure" into the Kingdom of God through Jesus and His ministers as described above.

The Other Purpose for Giving

The tithe was directed while offerings were meant to be given to the poor. Alms were clearly mentioned by Jesus in Matthew 6:1.

> *"Take heed that you do not do your charitable deeds before men, to be seen by them. Otherwise you have no reward from your Father in heaven. ² Therefore, when you do a charitable deed, do not sound a trumpet before you as the*

hypocrites do in the synagogues and in the streets, that they may have glory from men. Assuredly, I say to you, they have their reward. ³ But when you do a charitable deed, do not let your left hand know what your right hand is doing, ⁴ that your charitable deed may be in secret; and your Father who sees in secret will Himself reward you openly."

The offerings mentioned in II Cor. 8 were clearly to help the suffering in Jerusalem.

"1 Moreover, brethren, we make known to you the grace of God bestowed on the churches of Macedonia: ² that in a great trial of affliction the abundance of their joy and their deep poverty abounded in the riches of their liberality."

It also included an element of faith.

³ For I bear witness that according to their ability, yes, and beyond their ability, they were freely willing, ⁴ imploring us with much urgency that we would receive the gift and the fellowship of the ministering to the saints.

It demonstrated a fresh commitment to God.

> "*5 And not only as we had hoped, but they first gave themselves to the Lord, and then to us by the will of God.*"

And it showed a growth in grace.

> "*6 So we urged Titus, that as he had begun, so he would also complete this grace in you as well. 7 But as you abound in everything—in faith, in speech, in knowledge, in all diligence, and in your love for us—see that you abound in this grace also.*"

It was not a requirement for any individual II Cor.9.

> *5 Therefore I thought it necessary to exhort the brethren to go to you ahead of time, and prepare your generous gift beforehand, which you had previously promised, that it may be ready as a matter of generosity and not as a grudging obligation.*

Jesus certainly taught that it was right for a person to have certain personal values that guide his life. Luke 6:38 is one of those principles buried within a list of attitudes that a person should possess. This one was to have a giving spirit.

> *Luke 6:38 "³⁸Give, and it will be given to you: good measure, pressed down, shaken together, and running over will be put into your bosom. For with the same measure that you use, it will be measured back to you."*

Every tither and his pastor can quote this verse but almost never in context. It does not mention money but seems to mention a spirit that makes life better.

Malachi 3:8-10

> *⁸"Will a man rob God? Yet you have robbed Me! But you say, 'In what way have we robbed You?' In tithes and offerings. ⁹You are cursed with a curse, For you have robbed Me, Even this whole nation. ¹⁰Bring all the tithes into the storehouse, That there may be food in My house, And try Me now in this," Says the LORD of hosts, "If I will not open for you the windows of heaven And pour out for you such blessing That there will not be room enough to receive it."*

Is this for you and me today? The context seems to be to the priests who did not fulfill their obligation in performing the office of priest. Two logical questions occur to me as I read these verses. 1. Where is the curse? Everyone knows of Believers who have fallen into some sort of misfortune but in general there should be many, many who live cursed lives. 2. Where is the bounty? We all have stories of a God supplying our needs in unusual ways but in general there should be faithful tithers who have so much that they can't figure out what to do with it. I do know that the nation of Israel and especially the priests were cursed as they forgot God. The Old Testament ends that way, with God only able to find a remnant.

Malachi 3: "¹⁴ You have said, 'It is useless to serve God; What profit is it that we have kept His ordinance, And that we have walked as mourners Before the LORD of hosts? ¹⁵ So now we call the proud blessed, For those who do wickedness are raised up; They even tempt God and go free.'"

¹⁶ Then those who feared the LORD spoke to one another, And the LORD listened and heard them; So a book of remembrance was written before Him For those who fear the LORD And who meditate on His name."

Old Testament vs. New Testament Purpose

The question that started this whole process with me is "why is store house tithing so hard to justify in the New Testament?" Certainly God noticed the void. I began to ask more questions like, "what are the differences in the mission from Old to New?" I concluded that the Old Testament featured a small nation whose religious focus was on supporting one tribe of people, the Levites, and maintaining one building, the Temple. *Multiple ministries did not exist. Multiple Temples did not exist.* Not so today.

Today the scope of ministry is vastly bigger. The mission is global involving millions of ministers, millions of projects and millions of approaches to spreading the message of God. The "church" is universal. Every believer belongs to it. Every minister works to advance it, lifting up Jesus to the world. God does not live in a small building in Jerusalem anymore but lives within each of us. The solution is not a New Testament invention. In fact, the New Testament does not invent doctrine that cannot be found in demonstration form in the Old Testament. The pattern is found in the tithe.

If you build it, they will come?

The Great Commission tells us to *go* but the buildings that we build tell the world to *come*. I'm afraid that we have "built" away the urgency to carry the message around the world. In fact, church building did not show up on the Christian landscape until around 300 A.D. Before that the groups remained small meeting in any and every place they could. When Constantine had his "vision" and legalized Christianity, the "church" suddenly became a religion that must be "fit for a king." The king was not likely to visit your home for a small group meeting. As the "religion" evolved the government required "ministers" to be licensed and they were elevated above the common man. It actually became illegal for a non-licensed person to conduct a meeting to teach the Bible. The downward spiral began that corrupted the whole business of spreading the Gospel.

Today, of all Gospel dollars spent, 90 percent goes to minister to 5 percent of the world, Americans. Most of that money is spent on constructing buildings which seems to give the "church" a place to hide from the world. The imbalance is troubling to me. I see minister after minister who would carry the message outside of America, having to beg for financial help and often give up in despair.

The Old Testament Temple was built by special offerings collected for that purpose. There was only one but it seems fair that today's church can do the same based on the size of the congregation. I see no problem building a church building to house the people who want to come but I do see a problem if that is the highest prize. The congregation should build a building that they need and not one that they hope they will need in the future. Take an offering and build the building, but keep borrowing to a minimum. The apostles of Jesus were shocked when He did not hold their building, the Temple, in as high regard as they did. An imbalance exists today.

The fastest growing Christian movement in the world today is in China. House churches are springing up at the rate of 10,000 per month. All of this is done without permission of the government (it is illegal, with the threat of imprisonment) and without buildings. It can be done. There are more believers in China today than in the United States.

How should it work?

Jesus said in Matthew. 6:21

> *"21 For where your treasure is, there your heart will be also."*

God is able to put something on your heart, I John 3:

"[20] For if our heart condemn us, God is greater than our heart, and knows all things."

Where is your heart? For some people their hearts are burning for the church. Years ago, as a pastor, I knew of a man in the church who seemed to be giving an inordinate amount regularly. I called him into my office and questioned him about the large amount that he was giving to the church. He told me that he became a believer in that church, and that his wife became a believer in that church, and even his children became believers in that church. He told me that his children went to school in the school that we had established in that church, he thought that his children would probably find their life's' mates in that church and probably get married in that church. Furthermore, he thought that he would probably have his future funeral in that church. *It was clear that his heart was in that church.*

The hearts of some people are with a *foreign* ministry. Some want to see Bibles flown into foreign countries. Some think that beaming radio into forbidden lands is the greatest need. *You can see where this is going.* Shouldn't all of this be done through the local church? The "church" does not seem to have a good track record with regard to a balanced approach to global ministry. It is important for a person however to share in the local ministry where he is fed spiritually. Anything less would be akin to freeloading.

My New Conclusion

This is a total paradigm shift for me but I think that I have changed my mind. I hope that it is *not* because I am an independent minister.

1. Tithing is for today but not required to be given to the "storehouse" or church. The New Testament giving mentioned is only for alms. There is ***no other mechanism*** taught in the New Testament for spreading the Gospel to the world except for tithing.

2. Church buildings are to be funded by special offerings (not tithe) from the congregation. Good stewardship should be observed.

3. The church where you are fed and attend should be very high on your list for support.

4. Ministries around the world, fulfilling the Great Commission should be supported.

5. Poor people should be helped by individuals, from non tithe support.

Lordship Salvation

It is extremely common to hear someone refer to a person's salvation saying that he had accepted Jesus as his Lord and Savior. I hear it when one submits to baptism. I hear it when one refers to his own salvation. It has become common vernacular in many Christian circles today, but not without controversy. The two definitions below are taken directly from the internet and give fairly thorough explanations with bombastic inflammatory language, which I appreciate.

Lordship salvation is the position that receiving Christ involves a turning in the heart from sin and, as a part of faith, a submissive commitment to obey Jesus Christ as Lord. It also maintains that progressive sanctification (constantly being set apart for the use of God) and perseverance (one cannot lose his salvation) must necessarily follow conversion. Those who hold to the doctrine of perseverance of the saints see it not only as a requirement, but an assured certainty according to the sustaining grace of Christ.

The doctrine of lordship salvation has implications for evangelism, assurance, and the pursuit of holiness. The grace of God in salvation not only forgives, but transforms, and a lack of obedience or transformation in a person's life is warrant to doubt he has have been born again. The grounds for assurance include not only the objective promises of God (like John 3:16), but also the internal testimony of the   Spirit   (Romans   8:16)   and holiness the Spirit produces in our lives (1 John 2:3-4, 19).

The non-lordship salvation position is popularly known by critics as "easy believism", and by adherents as "free grace". However, proponents of Lordship salvation frown upon this usage of the term "free grace", as the free grace spoken of in the Bible both justifies the sinner *and* transforms the heart unto obedience.

Free Grace Theology is a soteriological (salvation) view teaching that everyone receives eternal life the moment he **believes** in Jesus Christ as his personal Savior and Lord. "Lord" refers to the belief that Jesus is the Son of God and therefore able to be his "Savior". The view distinguishes between the "call to believe" in Christ as a Savior and receiving the gift of eternal life, and the "call to follow" Christ and to become obedient disciples, meaning that the justified believer is *free* from any subsequent obligations unless he or she decides to undergo the process of sanctification.

In particular, the Gospel of John and most of the writings of Paul of Tarsus are seen by proponents as the overt Scriptural basis of *Free Grace theology*. A distinctive (and much debated) argument is that the Gospel of John is the only book in the New Testament with the stated purpose of providing the needed information for one to be born again. Another assertion is that Jesus Christ stated both explicitly (John 14:1, 14:27, Matthew 11:28) and implicitly (John 6:35, 6:37, Luke 10:41-2) that He "will give rest" to the believer, in contrast to a "troubled heart"

180

and a demand of "labor" before salvation.

The Bigger Picture.

Recently, I have come to the view that the New Testament does not create doctrine; it only amplifies and articulates it. All doctrine begins in the Old Testament and it is from there that we should go to answer tough doctrinal questions. We can see the doctrine of salvation demonstrated in the lives of the Old Testament believers and God's interaction with them. If we were to adopt that practice of looking for the Old Testament pattern, we could more easily solve much religious controversy.

Old Testament Examples.

The benchmark for "faith" in the Old Testament is found in Abraham (Gen. 15:6). In fact, several times in the New Testament salvation by faith was demonstrated in the life of Abraham, (Romans 4, Gal. 3, and Heb. 11).

> ***Romans 4:1*** *"What then shall we say that Abraham our father has found according to the flesh? ² For if Abraham was justified by works, he has something to boast about, but not before God.³ For what does the Scripture say? "Abraham believed God, and it was accounted to him for righteousness." ⁴ Now to him who works, the*

181

wages are not counted as grace but as debt. ⁵ But to him who does not work but believes on Him who justifies the ungodly, his faith is accounted for righteousness"

__Gal 3:__ "⁶ just as Abraham "believed God, and it was accounted to him for righteousness" ⁷ Therefore know that only those who are of faith are sons of Abraham. ⁸ And the Scripture, foreseeing that God would justify the Gentiles by faith, preached the gospel to Abraham beforehand, saying, "In you all the nations shall be blessed."] ⁹ So then those who are of faith are blessed with believing Abraham."

__Hebrews 11"__ ⁸ By faith Abraham obeyed when he was called to go out to the place which he would receive as an inheritance. And he went out, not knowing where he was going. ⁹ By faith he dwelt in the land of promise as in a foreign country, dwelling in tents with Isaac and Jacob, the heirs with him of the same promise; ¹⁰ for he waited for the city which has foundations, whose builder and maker is God."

Sarah, Abraham's wife, is notable for her saving faith, seeming to have a confident opinion about God (aka faith).

> **Hebrews 11** *"[11] By faith Sarah herself also received strength to conceive seed, and she bore a child when she was past the age, because she judged Him faithful who had promised."*

The characteristic found in the Old Testament believers seems to be a realization that God has something better and a desire for it which is honored by God.

> **Hebrew 11:** *"[13] These all died in faith, not having received the promises, but having seen them afar off were assured of them, embraced them and confessed that they were strangers and pilgrims on the earth. [14] For those who say such things declare plainly that they seek a homeland. [15] And truly if they had called to mind that country from which they had come out, they would have had opportunity to return. [16] But now they desire a better, that is, a heavenly country. Therefore God is not ashamed to be called their God, for He has prepared a city for them."*

Two Forks in the Road.

I see two forks in the road. The first fork asks us to make a saving choice to;

183

Come, Matthew. 11

"*28 Come to Me, all you who labor and are heavy laden, and 1 will give you rest. 29 Take My yoke upon you and learn from Me, for 1 am gentle and lowly in heart, and you will find rest for your souls. 30 For My yoke is easy and My burden is light.*"

Believe, John 3

"*16 For God so loved the world that He gave His only begotten Son, that whoever believes in Him should not perish but have everlasting life. 17 For God did not send His Son into the world to condemn the world, but that the world through Him might be saved. 18 "He who believes in Him is not condemned; but he who does not believe is condemned already, because he has not believed in the name of the only begotten Son of God.*"

Receive, John 1

"*11 He came to His own,[c] and His own[d] did not receive Him. 12 But as many as received Him, to them He gave the right to become children of God, to those who believe in His name*"

Repent, from unbelief Acts 2

> *36 "Therefore let all the house of Israel know assuredly that God has made this Jesus, whom you crucified, both Lord and Christ." 37 Now when they heard this, they were cut to the heart, and said to Peter and the rest of the apostles, "Men and brethren, what shall we do?" 38 Then Peter said to them, "Repent, and let every one of you be baptized in the name of Jesus Christ for the remission of sins; and you shall receive the gift of the Holy Spirit."*

Trust, Psalms 78

> *"21 Therefore the LORD heard this and was furious; So a fire was kindled against Jacob, And anger also came up against Israel, 22 Because they did not believe in God, And did not trust in His salvation."*

Know, John 17

> *"3 And this is eternal life, that they may know You, the only true God, and Jesus Christ whom You have sent."*

None of these verbs evokes the idea of effort, nor should they.

> *Ephesians 2:8-9 "⁸ For by grace you have been saved through faith, and that not of yourselves; it is the gift of God, ⁹ not of works, lest anyone should boast."*

The Other Fork

The other fork asks us to make decisions regarding our level of commitment to Jesus. As we respond positively to God's leading through Scripture, we start down the road to discipleship. We are asked to;

Follow, Matthew. 16

> *"24 Then Jesus said to His disciples, "If anyone desires to come after **Me**, let him deny himself, and take up his cross, and **follow Me**."*

Forsake, Luke 14

> *"33 So likewise, whoever of you does not **forsake** all that he has cannot be My disciple."*

Grow, Eph. 4

> *"¹⁴ that we should no longer be children, tossed to and fro and carried about with every wind of*

186

doctrine, by the trickery of men, in the cunning craftiness of deceitful plotting, [15] but, speaking the truth in love, may grow up in all things into Him who is the head—Christ—[16] from whom the whole body, joined and knit together by what every joint supplies, according to the effective working by which every part does its share, causes growth of the body for the edifying of itself in love."

Bear fruit, II Pet 1

"[5] But also for this very reason, giving all diligence, add to your faith virtue, to virtue knowledge, [6] to knowledge self-control, to self-control perseverance, to perseverance godliness, [7] to godliness brotherly kindness, and to brotherly kindness love. [8] For if these things are yours and abound, you will be neither barren nor unfruitful in the knowledge of our Lord Jesus Christ."

Win the lost, Matthew 21

[33] "Hear another parable: There was a certain landowner who planted a vineyard and set a hedge around it, dug a winepress in it and built a tower. And he leased it to vinedressers and went into a far country. [34] Now when vintage-

time drew near, he sent his servants to the vinedressers, that they might receive its fruit. *35* And the vinedressers took his servants, beat one, killed one, and stoned another. *36* Again he sent other servants, more than the first, and they did likewise to them. *37* Then last of all he sent his son to them, saying, 'They will respect my son.' *38* But when the vinedressers saw the son, they said among themselves, 'This is the heir. Come, let us kill him and seize his inheritance.' *39* So they took him and cast him out of the vineyard and killed him.

40 "Therefore, when the owner of the vineyard comes, what will he do to those vinedressers?"

41 They said to Him, "He will destroy those wicked men miserably, and lease his vineyard to other vinedressers who will render to him the fruits in their seasons."

42 Jesus said to them, "Have you never read in the Scriptures:

'The stone which the builders rejected Has become the chief cornerstone. This was the Lord's doing, and it is marvelous in our eyes"?
43 "Therefore I   say to you, the kingdom of

God will be taken from you and given to a nation bearing the fruits of it."

Obey, Luke 6

46 "But why do you call Me 'Lord, Lord,' and not do the things which I say?"

Hunger, Matthew 5

"6 Blessed are those who hunger and thirst for righteousness, For they shall be filled."

Turn from sin, Eph 4

"22 that you put off, concerning your former conduct, the old man which grows corrupt according to the deceitful lusts, 23 and be renewed in the spirit of your mind, 24 and that you put on the new man which was created according to God, in true righteousness and holiness. 25 Therefore, putting away lying, "Let each one of you speak truth with his neighbor," for we are members of one another."

Submit, James 4

"7 Therefore submit to God. Resist the devil and he will flee from you. 8 Draw near to God and He will

draw near to you. Cleanse your hands, you sinners; and purify your hearts, you double-minded. ⁹ Lament and mourn and weep! Let your laughter be turned to mourning and your joy to gloom. ¹⁰ Humble yourselves in the sight of the Lord, and He will lift you up."

EVERYTHING LISTED ABOVE

Everything listed above calls for "believers" to expand their commitment to God. The list would not even exist if a person, from the beginning, accepted Jesus as Lord and Savior. He would have initiated every step from the beginning. It seems apparent that there is a learning curve for believers and that they have to learn, yield, learn, yield. It is not likely that every person will follow each step at the same pace or even at all. We are all different. Some people have stronger will power to improve while some are not as disciplined. All of this growth can only take place IF a person does in fact learn and yield. He may do neither. He may grow later or not at all. Just as in the physical world, every child (of God) is different.

Isn't it just semantics?

There are inherent dangers in Lordship Salvation. The theology may actually keep an unbeliever from accepting the simple Gospel of Jesus. Gospel means "good news" looking too far down the road, to normal Christian struggles, may give Satan the opening needed to scare one off. One may view the whole process as "bad news." It certainly can look ominous. In my view, the list below presents some of the issues about Lordship Salvation.

First, Lordship Salvation changes the very heart of the Gospel, which only requires a child-like faith. There are probably somewhere between 150 to 200 New Testament passages which singularly condition a lost person's salvation upon belief alone in Christ (John 3:16; 6:28-29; Acts 16:31; Romans 1:16, etc...).

Second, Lordship Salvation places an impossible requirement upon the unsaved. The unsaved person is dead in his trespasses and sins (Eph 2:1) and thus incapable of doing anything of spiritual value, such as obey, submit, forsake, etc...By making these other things the conditions of salvation rather than simply believing, obstacles are placed in front of the unbeliever that he or she is incapable of fulfilling.

Third, Lordship Salvation ignores the possibility of a carnal Christian. If complete commitment and yielding to Christ is an initial prerequisite for salvation, then there is no such thing as a believer who is carnal or not completely surrendered to Christ. Yet the Bible contains numerous examples of carnal believers. For example, Lot, who is called "righteous" three times (2 Pet 2:7-8), exhibits perpetual unrighteous behavior (Gen 19:30-38). Similarly, the Corinthians are called saints (1 Cor 1:2), yet the rest of 1 Corinthians reveals their un-saintly behavior. Thus, Paul refers to them as carnal believers (1 Cor 3:1-3). While carnal Christianity is obviously not God's perfect will for His children, such a categorization is a legitimate possibility.

Fourth, Lordship Salvation confuses sanctification with justification. After coming to Christ, God issues another call for His children to pursue practical sanctification or discipleship. For example, those whom Christ called to be His disciples, like Peter, were already believers (Matthew 16:24-25). One great issue is how a person views "repentance." For an explanation, see the chapter on "repentance" in this book.

Fifth, Lordship Salvation destroys the believer's assurance of salvation. Lordship advocates never precisely define what kind of commitment to Christ is necessary in order to become a Christian. How much surrender is required? How long is this surrender to last? How much fruit must this surrender produce?

The only true test.

Unquestionably salvation brings about change in a persons life. The main problem is being able to discern what that change is. If a person is truly "born again," then a new spirit lives within him. An internal change has taken place but it may not be visible to man. God told us that His perspective is different from ours

I Sam. 16:7

> *"But the LORD said to Samuel, "Do not look at his **appearance** or at his physical stature, because I have refused him. For the LORD does not see as man sees; for man looks at the outward **appearance**, but the LORD looks at the heart."*

The most difficult question is how can we tell if a person is truly a believer? We cannot see the heart; only God can. In my opinion, the only way that we can tell if a person is a believer is not necessarily what he does differently but how differently does God treat him? In general, God does not judge lost men in this life but in the next. He is not willing that any should perish but that all should come to repentance. God will however judge the sin in the life of a believer. He loves His children too much to let them continue in sin. He expects growth. This is called discipleship. The only true test for a believer is, "will God let him get away with sin?"

Hebrews 12

> *"⁵And you have forgotten the exhortation which speaks to you as to sons:*

"My son, do not despise the chastening of the LORD, Nor be discouraged when you are rebuked by Him; ⁶For whom the LORD loves He chastens, And scourges every son whom He receives."

⁷If you endure chastening, God deals with you as with sons; for what son is there whom a father does not chasten? ⁸But if you are without chastening, of which all have become partakers, then you are illegitimate and not sons."

Yes, salvation makes a change in a person's life but it is not always visible.

Salvation is free, discipleship costs everything.

At the end of World War II, the allied forces lead by the United States military, under the command of General Douglas McArthur, exerted unimaginable force over their adversary, Japan, by dropping the atomic bomb. Finally, realizing that they were overpowered, Japan surrendered to the allied forces. The surrender ceremony was held on September 2, 1945 aboard the United States Naval battleship USS *Missouri*, at which officials from the Japanese government signed the Japanese Instrument of Surrender, thereby ending the hostilities in World War II.

Japan surrendered completely agreeing to every condition that was asked of them by the   superior power. From that day forward, Japan has prospered, even exceeding anything that they had ever imagined. Today they are a world financial and industrial power far beyond most industrial countries.

It all happened because they surrendered fully to a benevolent and superior authority. Is there a lesson there for us? *Salvation is free but full surrender to God will yield the fulfilled life.*

Divorce and Remarriage

Divorce in the Christian world is one of those things that always elicit emotional responses. Even in the world of Christian grace, those involved in divorce seem to get little. In fact, it appears that when the subject of divorce comes up, we always revert to the Law of Moses. Grace goes out the window.

A Dishonest Question.

In Matthew 19:1 Jesus was approach by some Pharisee leaders who were constantly trying to trick Him into a cultural or religious mistake.

> *"Now it came to pass, when Jesus had finished these sayings, that He departed from Galilee and came to the region of Judea beyond the Jordan. ² And great multitudes followed Him, and He healed them there.*
>
> *³ The Pharisees also came to Him, testing Him, and saying to Him, "Is it lawful for a man to divorce his wife for just any reason?"*
>
> *⁴ And He answered and said to them, "Have you not read that He who made them at the beginning 'made them male and female,' ⁵ and said, 'For this*

reason a man shall leave his father and mother and be joined to his wife, and the two shall become one flesh'? *6 So then, they are no longer two but one flesh. Therefore what God has joined together, let not man separate."*

7 They said to Him, "Why then did Moses command to give a certificate of divorce, and to put her away?"

8 He said to them, "Moses, because of the hardness of your hearts, permitted you to divorce your wives, but from the beginning it was not so. 9 And I say to you, whoever divorces his wife, except for sexual immorality, and marries another, commits adultery; and whoever marries her who is divorced commits adultery."

Several issues come to the fore in this dialogue. **First,** there existed within the culture of the Jews something called "any cause" divorce, which is the matter the Pharisees asked about. The eastern world was not very protective of the women. As time went on, men invented the "any cause" divorce to allow themselves to flit from one wife to another, in self gratification. Love, forgiveness and compassion were not the norm. Today in our western culture, we have certain practices and attitudes (supposedly) that create a more stable environment for women than exist in eastern cultures. Women have more rights in the western world for sure. Men are not generally allowed by our western laws and culture to abandon their wives. Not so in the distant history of Israel. By the time of Jesus men could "dump" their wives for "any cause" or even worse, do some physical harm to them. You can imagine the chaos that would be created in a society that did not have social and governmental safety nets for the women.

The correct answer by Jesus took them back to the very beginning, to the original intent of God. It is a great practice to find out theological and social answers by going back to God's original purpose and pattern. Paul expounded on the idea of the "two becoming one flesh" in Ephesians 5:28.

> *28 So husbands ought to love their own wives as their own bodies; he who loves his wife loves himself. 29 For no one ever hated his own flesh, but nourishes and cherishes it, just as the Lord does the church. 30 For we are members of His body, of His flesh and of His bones. 31 "For this reason a man shall leave his father and mother and be joined to his wife, and the two shall become one flesh."*

If a man were to think of his wife as a part of his own body he would surely manage his marriage better. Men take care of their bodies and should likewise take care of their wives. This rather makes a sham of the "any cause" divorce idea.

The **second** issue found within this seemingly simple question has to do with the Law of Moses. The Pharisees asked why Moses commanded a certificate of divorcement. *Moses did not command divorce.* The divorce that Moses allowed was designed to protect the wife from being summarily dismissed from the husband. In fact, Jesus told them that the *real cause* of their divorces was the hardness of their own hearts. Hardness of heart is a direct sin against God. Imagine these men divorcing their wives while all the time misdirecting the blame to them and at the same time carefully practicing their religion.   Interestingly enough, this chapter mentioning divorce immediately follows the chapter containing ideas on forgiveness and preceding dialogue about sinning against children.

I also find it interesting that men are so adept at "using" Scripture to justify their behavior. It seems very "human" to read the Bible and nit pick issues instead of stepping back to see the bigger picture. Men and women alike do it with great skill. Imagine a woman with-holding sex from her husband for months or even years, waiting for him to slip up and be caught in some indiscretion, in order for her to be justified in seeking divorce. The man of course would be considered a scoundrel to all of her friends. The men in our story were very good at "proof texting" rather   than   searching   for   God's purpose.

Thirdly, moral consequences are discussed with the Pharisees that should have given those hard-hearted men pause - adultery. It seems quite likely that the men to which the address is directed had already had "any cause" divorce, thus the hardness of "your" hearts. It even seems that the disciples were also engaged in such practices or at least they sought to cling to the option, Matthew. 19:10.

> *"10 His disciples said to Him, "If such is the case of the man with his wife, it is better not to marry."*

The Original Union

In Genesis 2, at the creation narrative, God declared that it was "not good" that man should be alone. He stated that man should have a helper. From that idea, it can be thought that man was not self sufficient, without need of anything. In fact, it seems that God created woman to fill some deficiency in man. I have often wondered why men and women are so different, what was God thinking when he did that? Clearly we are not the same. Books have been written about the glaring differences in man from woman. From my own experience I have noticed that I am task oriented. When "on task," nothing else seems to matter to me. Normal human relationships are set aside, emotion is tabled. My wife however, is more likely to remember one of my grandkids birthdays, with which I am oblivious. If it were not for my wife, I would stay in trouble with some of my ordinary familial relationships. She completes me in that way.

In the beginning of our human relationships, several features stand out.

1. Man and woman were not spoken into existence. The act was much more intimate.

2. Man and woman were one before they were two with the woman being taken out of man.

3. No option for divorce existed before the fall or even very long after. The notion was clearly a result of the fall, and the "hardness of heart."

4. Marriage is physical not civil. In our western culture, we tend to think of marriage as a union established by some civil authority. Globally however, such civil unions may not exist. Marriage to me is the union of sex as attested by Paul, I Cor. 6:16

> *"16 Or do you not know that he who is joined to a harlot is one body with her? For "the two," He says, "shall become one flesh."*

5. God instituted marriage, not the state. The "state" did not even exist when the institute was begun. Even though "man" may grant divorce, God does not accept it, Mark 10:9.

"⁹ Therefore what God has joined together, let not man separate."

6. The union should be closer than with mother and father,

Gen. 2:24

> *"²⁴ Therefore a man shall leave his father and mother and be joined to his wife, and they shall become one flesh."*

7. There is a bigger picture than a mere physical union. In Ephesians 5, as Paul is instructing men and women on their marital relationships, he makes a startling statement, declaring a mystery, Eph. 5:32.

> *"³² This is a great mystery, but I speak concerning Christ and the church."*

The Bigger Picture.

With God, nothing is simple. I would be surprised if anything of importance only had one layer to it i.e.

* Moses hitting the rock, Exodus

* The Passover

* Abraham's delay in having a son

* Abraham's meeting with Melchizedek

* God covering Adam and Eve with skin after the fall

* Jesus passing through Samaria for water

* etc, etc, etc and many more

In Ephesians 5:32, mentioned above, a picture is drawn linking marriage to the relationship of Christ to the church. Certainly that idea did not occur to God later in time but was His intent all along, from the beginning. God asked the prophet Hosea to marry a harlot in order to demonstrate His feelings about the way Israel had treated their relationship with God, Hosea 1.

> *"2 When the LORD began to speak by Hosea, the LORD said to Hosea: "Go, take yourself a wife of harlotry and children of harlotry, For the land has committed great harlotry By departing from the LORD."*

The relation between Christ and the church (believers) is depicted by marriage and marriage is depicted by the relationship between Christ and the church. The structure should be the same. There are certain characteristics between the two that MUST be noted and followed, Ephesians 5.

> *"22 Wives, submit to your own husbands, as to the Lord. 23 For the husband is head of the wife, as*

also Christ is head of the church; and He is the Savior of the body. 24 Therefore, just as the church is subject to Christ, so let the wives be to their own husbands in everything. 25 Husbands, love your wives, just as Christ also loved the church and gave Himself for her, 26 that He might sanctify and cleanse her with the washing of water by the word, 27 that He might present her to Himself a glorious church, not having spot or wrinkle or any such thing, but that she should be holy and without blemish. 28 So husbands ought to love their own wives as their own bodies; he who loves his wife loves himself. 29 For no one ever hated his own flesh, but nourishes and cherishes it, just as the Lord does the church. 30 For we are members of His body, of His flesh and of His bones. 31 "For this reason a man shall leave his father and mother and be joined to his wife, and the two shall become one flesh." 32 This is a great mystery, but I speak concerning Christ and the church. 33 Nevertheless let each one of you in particular so love his own wife as himself, and let the wife see that she respects her husband."

1. Wives submit. This is not a popular concept in the western world today and that might explain many divorces. Wives should make this idea part of their   consideration in accepting the

marriage proposal. This understanding should be taken into marriage. It could come from premarital counseling but should certainly be observed by children as they see it played out in their homes between husbands and wives. It is too often NOT the case in today's society.

2. Husbands love wives. If that were the case in Matthew 19, I wonder if the question would have been asked about divorce.

3. Love is to be demonstrated. Jesus made a significant investment into the church even though the church was not perfect. It would be easy for a husband to devote himself to a perfect wife, but an imperfect? Much more difficult but nevertheless required.

4. Marriage should be a perfecting relationship. Even though man is imperfect, part of his purpose should be to develop and grow, moving toward the perfect, though not able to achieve it in this life. Nothing should be static about this relationship. Both husband and wife should be becoming better people, just as in the sanctification process. The Word of God is the tool to be used here not the will of the husband, but the Father.

5. The husband should treat his wife as his own flesh. If the wife submits, this is easier than if the wife resists the authority of the husband. A man's body generally does not rebel against him.

6. Jesus never casts out the church, never divorces the church. Hosea was not allowed to divorce Gomer but love and forgive her.

Matthew Henry, in his famous commentary from years gone by, succinctly describes the issue.

> *"The law of Moses allowing divorce for the hardness of men's hearts, and the law of Christ forbidding it, intimate, that Christians being under a dispensation of love and liberty, tenderness of heart may justly be expected among them, that they will not be hard-hearted, like Jews, for God has called us to peace. There will be no occasion for divorces, if we forbear one another, and forgive one another, in love, as those that are, and hope to be, forgiven, and have found God not forward to put us away, Isa 50:1.*

> *Thus says the LORD:*

> *"Where is the certificate of your mother's divorce, Whom I have put away? Or which of My creditors is it to whom I have sold you? For your iniquities you have sold ourselves, And for your transgressions your mother has been put away.*

> *divorces, if husbands love*

their wives, and wives be obedient to their husbands, and they live together as heirs of the grace of life: and these are the laws of Christ, such as we find not in all the law of Moses."

Three Greek Words.

Part of the struggle of maintaining marriage is a misunderstanding of the word love as well as the expectations of marriage. Three Greek words are interpreted into English as love that describe matters of human relationships.

EROS is the word used for erotic or sensual responses to members of the opposite sex. Eros is not a bad thing, in fact God invented Eros. In my opinion, Eros is the first response that members of the opposite sex have to each other. It is the initial attraction. Eros also produces a chemical in the brain called dopamine. Dopamine is a neuron-transmitter that is produced by extreme pleasure. It actually can become addictive. With tongue in cheek, I think that it has been aptly named because it can turn one into a "dope." A person will become unable to think rationally when overloaded with this pleasure seeking chemical. Any adult knows, however, that the erotic love that husband and wives share is less of the driving force than it was during adolescence. That kind of love is *self-serving* and is not strong enough to hold a relationship together. Unfortunately too many marriages are based on that kind of love. When it diminishes, many people will think that they are no longer in love and self-justify a divorce.

PHILEO is another Greek word describing love. This one describes a social fondness that people have between themselves. Two people find that they have something in common and they are drawn to each other, meeting their social needs. This love is also *self-serving* and is likewise not strong enough to maintain a marriage. Interests change over the years and some people will say that they and their spouse "grew apart" and also justify a divorce.

AGAPE is the deepest kind of love described in the Greek language and has it's own characteristics. This is a Godly love as described in I John 4:7.

> *"7 Beloved, let us love one another, for love is of God; and everyone who loves is born of God and knows God. 8 He who does not love does not know God, for God is love. 9 In this the love of God was manifested toward us, that God has sent His only begotten Son into the world, that we might live through Him. 10 In this is love, not that we loved God, but that He loved us and sent His Son to be the propitiation for our sins. 11 Beloved, if God so loved us, we also ought to love one another."*

The indication is that one cannot even have this love

209

unless he has been born of God (born again – John 3). This is not a natural love as are EROS and PHILEO. In fact this kind of love must be chosen "let us love." If it can be directed, then it can either be obeyed or rejected. Jesus told His disciples that He was issuing another command to them, John 15:12.

> *"12 This is My commandment, that you love one another as I have loved you."*

A command can either be obeyed or disobeyed; therefore this love can either be chosen or rejected. The main difference is that this kind of love is NOT *self serving*. It is the kind of love that prompted Jesus to give of Himself, even dying for us (the church). Once a person understands and chooses AGAPE love for their spouse, love that is NOT *self-serving,* that person will be much less likely to use lame excuses for divorce.

Peter and Jesus

In John 21, Jesus has His famous dialogue with Peter centered on the subject of love.

> *"15 So when they had eaten breakfast, Jesus said to Simon Peter, "Simon, son of Jonah, do you love Me more than these?" He said to Him, "Yes, Lord; You know that I love You." He said to him, "Feed My lambs." 16 He said to him again a second time, "Simon, son of Jonah, do you love*

Me?" He said to Him, "Yes, Lord; You know that I love You." He said to him, "Tend My sheep."

¹⁷ He said to him the third time, "Simon, son of Jonah, do you love Me?" Peter was grieved because He said to him the third time, "Do you love Me?" And he said to Him, "Lord, You know all things; You know that I love You." Jesus said to him, "Feed My sheep.

¹⁸ Most assuredly, I say to you, when you were younger, you girded yourself and walked where you wished; but when you are old, you will stretch out your hands, and another will gird you and carry you where you do not wish." ¹⁹ This He spoke, signifying by what death he would glorify God. And when He had spoken this, He said to him, "Follow Me."

Since Peter was about to launch the church (the bride of Christ) on the Day of Pentecost and since Jesus is the bridegroom, it seems to me that the above dialogue might be seen as a marriage proposal. Jesus was certainly measuring Peter's commitment and causing him to take an inner look at his own heart. Did Peter express the kind of love strong enough for what would come? Jesus told Peter that his commitment would cost him his life. This is how marriage should work; a commitment that is life long and deep enough to overcome all trials and struggles.

Now we have come full circle with the Ephesians 5 instructions concerning the marriage relationship. The example, once again is Christ and the church, a marriage that CANNOT be broken - the pattern for marriage. However, we are not perfect like Jesus; we are sinners and will therefore have struggles with self interest and selfish desires. Just know that God does not offer you a way out of your marriage commitment but instead offers a way for two people to be led by the Spirit, yielding the fruits of the Spirit which make both sinners lovable.

Today's Christian Culture

To the non-Christian world, marriage has been cheapened, even to the point that it is becoming popular for same sex people to marry - how utterly ridiculous. How disgraceful to take an institution, owned by God, designed by God to picture an incredible spiritual union, and destroy its purpose and significance.

To the Christian world, marriage has seemingly become a union of convenience lasting as long as the "love shall last," whatever that means. With divorce always looming as an option, marriage commitments are naturally watered down.

It is my decision not to discuss any conditions that allow for divorce here. It would open the door a crack, allowing for Satan to stick his foot in and pry it open. No-one wants people to suffer but please acknowledge that some suffering is self imposed. The wonderful person that you married may have turned bad with your help. Whatever reason that you find to justify divorce, know that the REAL reason is "hardness of heart."

To Drink or Not to Drink – Alcohol

That certainly seems to be a good question. It seems that there are several thought processes from believers regarding the subject of drinking alcohol. Some people have no compunction at all and drink without controversy. Some people drink and have some inner feelings about the issue and constantly talk about it. They seem to always look for justification even if it means "protesting too loudly." Some people feel terrible about it and would never drink around other believers. There are many who are selective about whom they tell that they drink, they try to live in two different worlds. The group to which I am addressing is those who use the Bible to say that drinking is ok. After all, didn't Jesus turn water into wine?

As usual, advocates from both sides use the same scripture to justify both sides of the argument.

Arguments

Jesus turned water into wine.

Did Jesus turn water into "alcoholic" wine at a party?

Did Jesus drink alcoholic wine? It is assumed by a great many that He did. Let's examine this for a moment. Do you know how much wine Jesus made during His first miracle at the wedding feast of Cana? He made 6 firkins, or about 150 gallons. The New International Version (NIV) says by implication that Jesus did this "after the GUESTS had too much to drink". This version supposes that Jesus was at a party where the guests were drinking to excess, Jesus was one of the guests, and He supplied a few extra kegs to liven things up a bit after they had already drank to excess. Does that sound right to you?

Jesus Sinned?

The King James Bible (KJB) rendering which states they had "well drunken" (had plenty to drink) is the correct one. The New American Standard Version and other literal modern versions agree with the KJB here, leaving the NIV alone in its radically liberal paraphrase. Even if you take the rendering in the KJB, which I do, you have to conclude the guests had drunk their fill of wine. If this wine was alcoholic then it is likely that they would not be ready for another 150 gallons of alcoholic wine. Think about it. How many glasses of wine would this be? If you figure 4 ounces to a glass, 128 ounces to a gallon, you get 32 glasses of wine per gallon and a grand total of 4,800 glasses of wine. Now I do not know how many people were at this feast, but surely 500 would be a large number for such an event at this time. If this wine was alcoholic then Jesus did cause all who were there to drink to excess. Proverbs chapters 20 and 23 certainly call the use of alcohol unwise. I wouldn't like to think that Jesus was not wise. Not only would His excessive drinking have been a sin, but

216

causing others to do so is also a sin. Every Jew present at this wedding, and they were undoubtedly all Jews, would have known Him to be a sinner because of this verse. Does that sound like Jesus, the sinless savior of the world?

Jesus drank alcohol?

Jesus was accused by the Pharisees of being a drunkard.

> *Matthew. 11: "[18] For John came neither eating nor drinking, and they say, 'He has a demon.' [19] The Son of Man came eating and drinking, and they say, 'Look, a glutton and a winebibber, a friend of tax collectors and sinners!' But wisdom is justified by her children."*

The argument as implied by Jesus is that since John did not have a demon, neither was Jesus a glutton or a winebibber. It was very common of the Pharisees to try to trap or accuse Jesus into making a doctrinal mistake or acting unwisely. It never happened.

The Passover Argument

It is argued that since Jesus observed Passover with His disciples that he certainly drank wine with them which was a part of the Passover practice. Interesting language is used in the Scripture that seems to say otherwise   regarding alcohol.

217

Mark 14: "*²²And as they were eating, Jesus took bread, blessed and broke it, and gave it to them and said, "Take, eat; this is My body."²³ Then He took the cup, and when He had given thanks He gave it to them, and they all drank from it. ²⁴ And He said to them, "This is My blood of the new covenant, which is shed for many. ²⁵ Assuredly, I say to you, I will no longer drink of the fruit of the vine until that day when I drink it new in the kingdom of God."*

The Bible certainly says much about drinking wine, even alcohol.

Priests forbidden

Leviticus 10: "*⁸ Then the LORD spoke to Aaron, saying: ⁹ "Do not drink wine or intoxicating drink, you, nor your sons with you, when you go into the tabernacle of meeting, lest you die. It shall be a statute forever throughout your generations, ¹⁰ that you may distinguish between holy and unholy, and between unclean and clean, ¹¹ and that you may teach the children of Israel all the statutes which the LORD has spoken to them by the hand of Moses."*

Nazirite vow to separate himself

218

Num. 6: 2 "Speak to the children of Israel, and say to them: 'When either a man or woman consecrates an offering to take the vow of a Nazirite, to separate himself to the LORD, ³ he shall separate himself from wine and similar drink; he shall drink neither vinegar made from wine nor vinegar made from similar drink; neither shall he drink any grape juice, nor eat fresh grapes or raisins. ⁴ All the days of his separation he shall eat nothing that is produced by the grapevine, from seed to skin."

Wine is a mocker

Prov. 20:1 "Wine is a mocker, Strong drink is a brawler, And whoever is led astray by it is not wise."

Wine/ strong drink impairs judgment.

Prov. 31: ⁴ "It is not for kings, O Lemuel, It is not for kings to drink wine, Nor for princes intoxicating drink; ⁵ Lest they drink and forget the law,
And pervert the justice of all the afflicted."

Wine may impair your passions

Isaiah 5: 11"Woe to those who rise early in the morning, That they may follow intoxicating drink; Who continue until night, till wine inflames them!"

Without question, God commands believers to avoid drunkenness (Ephesians 5:18). The Bible condemns drunkenness and its effects (Proverbs 23:29-35). Christians are also commanded to not allow their bodies to be "mastered" by anything (1 Corinthians 6:12; 2 Peter 2:19). Furthermore, drinking alcohol in excess is undeniably addictive. Scripture also forbids people of faith from doing anything that might offend other weaker brothers or encourage them to sin against their conscience (1 Corinthians 8:9-13). In light of these principles, it would be extremely difficult for any follower of Jesus to say he is drinking alcohol to the glory of God (1 Corinthians 10:31).

In New Testament times, the water was not very clean. Without modern sanitation, the water was often filled with bacteria, viruses, and all kinds of contaminants. The same is true in many third-world countries today. As a result, people often drank wine (or grape juice) because it was far less likely to be contaminated. In 1Timothy 5:23, Paul was instructing Timothy to stop drinking the water (which was probably causing his stomach problems) and instead drink wine. In that day, wine was fermented (containing alcohol), but not necessarily to the degree it is today. It is incorrect to say that it was all grape juice, but it is also incorrect to say that it was the

220

same thing as the wine commonly used today.

Better questions

Instead of asking "does the Bible support drinking" perhaps we could ask better questions such as: *Why* did Bible people drink wine? How long would it take for grape juice to begin fermenting? What is the alcohol content of fermented grape juice? Did wine have effects other then making one lose his senses? What was "mixed" wine? What does Jewish tradition allow regarding alcohol? What are the effects of drinking alcoholic beverages? Is there a correlation between today's alcohol and the wine of the Bible?

Why did they drink wine?

Golda Meir, 4th prime minister of Israel from 1969 to 1974, once famously said "why did God curse us with no water?" According to a Jewish government website;

> *"Water is considered as a national resource of utmost importance. Water is vital to ensure the population's well-being and quality of life and to preserve the rural-agricultural sector. Israel has suffered from a chronic water shortage for years. In recent years however, the situation has developed into a crisis so severe that it is feared that by the next summer it may be difficult to*

221

adequately supply municipal and household water requirements. The current cumulative deficit in Israel's renewable water resources amounts to approximately 2 billion cubic meters, an amount equal to the annual consumption of the State. The deficit has also lead to the qualitative deterioration of potable aquifer water resources that have, in part, become either of brackish quality or otherwise become polluted."

With today's technology, water is a big problem for the nation of Israel. What would have been the case in ancient times? In Florida, every time that a well is dug it produces water. In Israel, Jacob's well from the books of Genesis and John (4) was actually 135 feet deep dug by hand. It still produces water today and is a very famous tourist stop. I wonder how long it took to dig the well. I wonder how many other wells were dug that did not produce water.

If good water was not easily accessible in ancient Israel, what would they have to drink? What are the choices? They drank WINE from grapes. There was no other choice. In fact as the wine began to ferment it could be mixed with poor quality water and it would kill some of the parasites in the water making the water safer to drink.

Fermentation

Naturally (no additives) fermented wine has a low alcoholic content. Until the advent of widely available granulated sugar, strongly alcoholic wine was rare. To make wine strongly alcoholic like what we have today (10%-15%) you must add a lot of sugar and yeast. These are the two key components to fermentation, and they are not present in large enough quantities naturally to create the strong wine we have today. Alcoholic wine during biblical times, which was much weaker than the wine of today, was often watered down for drinking. They basically only had water and wine. Like Pepsi or Coke today, wine was consumed by adults and children alike as a tasty substitute for water. Watering down wine was something they did and they drank it this way regularly. Also, boiling it down to make syrup was frequently done for preservation. This boiling killed the yeast that would cause fermentation. The syrup could easily be reconstituted later for drinking purposes. A third form of preservation was by straining out the yeast to prevent fermentation. Preservation was important. A harvest of grapes was seasonal.

In the story of the Good Samaritan, Luke 10, wine was poured into the injured man's wounds providing a medicinal solution for killing germs. It seemed to work well and was understood by the hearers of the parable as an antiseptic. Obviously it had "some" alcohol content.

The word wine

It must be noted that the word wine has several meanings and must be properly exegeted. Any basic student of scripture knows that.

The word "wine" is mentioned 231 times in the King James Bible. In the Old Testament there are 3 Hebrew words that are all translated as "wine".

* YAYIN: Intoxicating, fermented wine (*Genesis 9:21*).

* TIROSH: Fresh grape juice (*Proverbs 3:10*).

* SHAKAR: Intoxicating, intensely alcoholic, strong drink (often referred to other intoxicants than wine) (*Numbers 28:7*).

The New Testament, translated from Greek, uses the word "wine" for both fermented and unfermented drink. There are 2 Greek words for wine the New Testament.

* OINOS: Wine (generic) – (*Matthew 9:17*)
-- unfermented, (*Mark 2:22)*
-- fermented. (Ephesians 5:18)

* GLEUKOS: Sweet wine, fresh juice (*Acts 2:13*).

Only people who are trying to prove an idea would intermingle the words indiscriminately.

Ethyl Alcohol aka Ethanol

A Wikipedia summary of the history of alcohol is very interesting.

> *The fermentation of sugar into ethanol is one of the earliest biotechnologies employed by humans. The intoxicating effects of ethanol consumption have been known since ancient times. Ethanol has been used by humans since prehistory as the intoxicating ingredient of alcoholic beverages. Dried residue on a 9,000 year old pottery shard, found in China, imply that Neolithic people consumed alcoholic beverages.*

> *Although distillation was well known by the early Greeks and Arabs, the first recorded production of alcohol from distilled wine was by the School of Salerno alchemists in the 12th century.*

It should be noted that nature NEVER forms spirituous liquors. The fruit (grape) may rot and turn sour but it takes SKILL to convert juice to alcohol. The indispensable conditions for vinous fermentation are exact proportions of sugar, yeast or gluten and water with air temperature between 50 and 75 degrees. It takes great skill after much experimentation for mankind to be able to form what God did not.

> *Proverbs 23:29 Who has woe? Who has sorrow? Who has contentions? Who has complaints? Who*

*has wounds without cause? Who has redness of eyes? [30] Those who linger long at the wine, Those who go in search of **mixed wine**.*

It is apparent that today's alcohol and the wine of Biblical times have nothing in common except for man's divisive manipulation. I actually doubt that Noah got drunk on purpose. I think that fermentation was something new to Noah as the entire ecology changed from the flood. Things certainly tended to "wind down" (entropy) faster after the flood. What is fermentation if not simple aging? The average age mentioned in the Bible prior to the flood was 850. After the flood, 120 was considered old.

Jewish Tradition

Although Jewish tradition does not determine the course of Bible believers (it was Jewish tradition that caused Jesus to be crucified), it is interesting to make observations about it regarding alcohol and wine.

Jewish tradition website:

In the Scriptures, wine is described as "bringing joy to G-d and man" (Judges 9:13). And, indeed, every sacrifice offered in the Holy Temple was accompanied by a wine libation. Because wine is considered to be the "king of beverages" the rabbis coined a special blessing to be recited exclusively on wine: the Hagafenblessing.

And let us not forget the venerated age-old Jewish custom to say "l'chaim" and wish each other well over a shot glass of Schnapps.

Conversely, we are told of the destructive nature of wine and intoxication. Several examples:

According to an opinion expressed in the Talmud, the "Tree" of Knowledge was actually a grapevine. Thus it was the fruit of the vine that tripped up Adam and Eve, causing them and their descendents untold hardship and misery.[1]

The righteous Noah, whose righteousness caused G-d to spare the human race, was disgraced by excessive wine consumption.

Nadab and Abihu, Aaron's two holy sons, entered the Tabernacle while drunk and were consumed by a fire that emanated from the heavens.

The Torah extols the virtue, courage, and holiness of the Nazirite who vows to abstain from wine.

So what is wine? Is it a holy beverage with immense powers, reserved for holy and special occasions? Or is it a destructive agent with the power to bring down mighty people; a substance to be avoided at all costs?

Well, a little bit of both, it seems. As we mentioned earlier, according to one opinion, the Tree of Knowledge was a grape vine—and the Tree of Knowledge is dubbed by the Torah as being "good and bad." It has tremendous potential, when utilized properly, and a drawback of equal proportion, if misused and abused. What we use it for is entirely up to us.

Wine's ability to bring joy is because it relaxes our inhibitions and weakens the body's natural defenses. This "weakening of the body" allows the soul to shine through. After taking a l'chaim, one is more easily inspired because the body offers less resistance. This obviously applies only when one drinks in moderation and on special, holy occasions in an attempt to make them a bit more festive and to introduce an inspirational ambiance.

On the other hand, getting drunk in order to escape responsibilities we have to ourselves, to our families, and to those around us, is highly destructive. A person who is in an "escapist" mode is a dangerous person, because very often he is also escaping many of the rules that he would be wise to follow.

On the practical side, we are forbidden to pray while drunk and priests were not allowed to serve in the Holy

Temple whilst drunk. Even today, priests may not bless the congregation after having even a single glass of wine.

ONCE AGAIN, the wine of the Bible has nothing to do with the wine mentioned from the Jewish web site. Noah never heard of Schnapps.

Effects of Alcohol

Alcohol (which has nothing to do with the wine mentioned in the Bible), like marijuana, is considered a gateway drug by the United States Government Food and Drug Administration. The gateway leads to other drugs and things which are very unpleasant. The list below demonstrates what some of the consequences are for entering that gateway. For those people who advocate the use of alcohol, I have a question. Since alcohol and marijuana are first cousins as gateway drugs, why not take a hit of marijuana? In the places where it is legal in America, why not just go ahead and partake. Some day in the near future our government may recognize marijuana as a great source of tax revenue and like alcohol begin to tax it. Take a look at the list of effects below and ask yourself why anyone would go through the gate to begin with.

Alcohol causes 20 to 50 percent of all cirrhosis cases
Alcohol poisoning
Traffic accidents
Violence, assaults and murders

229

*Fetal alcohol syndrome disorder resulting in learning disabilities, social disabilities or at its worst, severe mental disabilities

*Unwanted pregnancies and sexually transmitted diseases due to risky sexual activity

*Serious withdrawal symptoms including hallucinations and seizures that can be fatal

*Epilepsy

*Pancreatitis

*Cancers of the colorectal, breast, larynx, liver, esophagus, oral cavity and pharynx

*Suicide

*Trauma and injury from falls, burns and assaults

*Drownings

*Cardiovascular disease

*Diabetes

Negative results from heavy alcohol use are routinely higher for men than for women. For example, in 2004, 6.2 percent of men's deaths were attributable to alcohol but only 1.1 percent of women's deaths. Young men are particularly prone to accidental death related to alcohol abuse.

Intoxication risks *(a study from one country only – Australia)*

Intoxication is the most common cause of alcohol-

related problems, leading to injuries and premature deaths. As a result, intoxication accounts for two-thirds of the years of life lost from drinking. Alcohol is responsible for:

30% of road accidents

44% of fire injuries

34% of falls and drownings

16% of child abuse cases

12% of suicides

10% of industrial accidents.

As well as deaths, short-term effects of alcohol result in illness and loss of work productivity (eg hangovers, drunken driving offences). In addition, alcohol contributes to criminal behavior - in 2010 it was reported that more than 70,000 Australians were victims of alcohol-related assault, among which 24,000 were victims of alcohol-related domestic violence.

Long-term effects

Each year approximately 3000 people die as a result of excessive alcohol consumption and around 100,000 people are hospitalized. Long-term excessive alcohol consumption is associated with:

*heart damage

*high blood pressure and stroke

*liver disease

*cancers of the digestive system

*other digestive system disorders (eg stomach ulcers)

*sexual impotence and reduced fertility

*increasing risk of breast cancer

*sleeping difficulties

*brain damage with mood and personality changes

*concentration and memory problems

*nutrition-related conditions

*risks to unborn babies

In addition to health problems, alcohol also impacts relationships, finances, work, and may result in legal problems.

At the most serious end, we found that in a given year, 367 Australians die because of another's drinking, and 13,660 are hospitalized. An estimated 19,443 substantiated child protection cases involve a carer's drinking and 24,581 assaults on family members reported to the police involve drinking, as do 44,852 assaults on the street and elsewhere.

In terms of the broader picture, most of us – 73% of adults – have experienced some kind of adverse effect in the last year from someone else's drinking. Of these, 5% were negatively affected in our work by a co-worker's drinking, 16% by a relative's or household member's drinking, 11% by a friend's and 43% when a stranger's drinking resulted in abuse, *threat, property damage or worse.*

But though adverse effects of strangers' drinking were more widely reported, the adverse effects in the household and family were more likely to be substantial, whether measured in terms of seriousness or of out-of-pocket costs and lost time from work."

World Medical Association - quote

*Alcohol use is deeply embedded in many societies. Overall, 4% of the global burden of disease is attributable to alcohol, which accounts for about as much death and disability globally as tobacco or hypertension.

*Alcohol-related problems are the result of a complex interplay between individual use of alcoholic beverages and the surrounding cultural, economic, physical environment, political and social contexts.

*Alcohol cannot be considered an ordinary beverage or consumer commodity since it is a drug that causes substantial medical, psychological and social harm by means of physical toxicity, intoxication and dependence. There is increasing evidence that genetic vulnerability to alcohol dependence is a risk factor for some individuals. Fetal alcohol syndrome and fetal alcohol effects, preventable causes of mental retardation, may

result from alcohol consumption during pregnancy.

*Alcohol advertising and promotion is rapidly expanding throughout the world and is increasingly sophisticated and carefully targeted, including to youth. It is aimed to attract, influence, and recruit new generations of potential drinkers despite industry codes of self-regulation that are widely ignored and often not enforced.

*Alcohol problems are highly correlated with per capita consumption so that reductions of use can lead to decreases in alcohol problems. Because alcohol is an economic commodity, alcohol beverage sales are sensitive to prices, i.e., as prices increase, demand declines, and visa versa. Price can be influenced through taxation and effective penalties for inappropriate sales and promotion activities. Such policy measures affect even heavy drinkers, and they are particularly effective among young people.

*Heavy drinkers and those with alcohol-related problems or alcohol dependence cause a significant share of the problems resulting from consumption. However, in most countries, the majority of alcohol-related problems in a population are associated with harmful or hazardous drinking by non-dependent 'social' drinkers, particularly when intoxicated. This is particularly a problem of young people in many regions of the world who drink with the intent of becoming intoxicated.

Although research has found some limited positive health effects of low levels of alcohol consumption in some populations, this must be weighed against potential harms from consumption in those same populations as well as in population as a whole.

Thus, population-based approaches that affect the social drinking environment and the availability of alcoholic beverages are more effective than individual approaches (such as education) for preventing alcohol related problems and illness. Alcohol policies that affect drinking patterns by limiting access and by discouraging drinking by young people through setting a minimum legal purchasing age are especially likely to reduce harms. Laws to reduce permitted blood alcohol levels for drivers and to control the number of sales outlets have been effective in lowering alcohol problems.

In recent years some constraints on the production, mass marketing and patterns of consumption of alcohol have been weakened and have resulted in increased availability and accessibility of alcoholic beverages and changes in drinking patterns across the world. This has created a global health problem that urgently requires governmental, citizen, medical and health care intervention.

Public Health and Regulatory Policies, Centre for Addiction and Mental Health, Toronto, ON, Canada.

I find it interesting that governments warn against

alcohol use while Christians, believers, followers of Jesus, Bible believing people of faith try so very hard to **justify** its use. I wonder if the level of justification is in any way related to the level of commitment to Jesus.

Some people actually relate alcohol to food, "everything in moderation." I have, however, never seen a person in prison for gluttony.

Biblical Warnings

Keep in mind that the wine of the Bible has no correlation with the alcohol of today's society. Today's alcohol is many times more potent than the "mixed wine" of the Bible. The warnings should be multiplied accordingly.

75 WARNINGS

There is more Scripture condemning the use of alcoholic beverages than will be found on the subjects of lying, adultery, swearing, cheating, hypocrisy, pride, or even blasphemy.

1) Genesis 9:20-26 - Noah became drunk; the result was immorality and family trouble.

2) Genesis 19:30-38 - Lot was so drunk he did not know what he was doing; this led to immorality

3) Leviticus 10:9-11 - God commanded priests not to drink so that they could tell the difference between the holy and the unholy.

4) Numbers 6:3 - The Nazarites were told to eat or drink nothing from the grape vine.

5) Deuteronomy 21:20 - A drunken son was stubborn and rebellious.

6) Deuteronomy 29:5-6 - God gave no grape juice to Israel nor did they have intoxicating drink in the wilderness.

7) Deuteronomy 32:33 - Intoxicating wine is like the poison of serpents, the cruel venom of asps.

8) Judges 13:4, 7, 14 - Samson was to be a Nazarite for life. His mother was told not to drink wine or strong drink.

9) 1 Samuel 1:14-15 - Accused, Hannah said she drank no wine.

10) 1 Samuel 25:32-38 - Nabal died after a drunken spree.

11) 2 Samuel 11:13 - By getting Uriah drunk, David hoped to cover his sin.

12) 2 Samuel 13:28-29 - Amnon was drunk when he was killed.

13) 1 Kings 16:8-10 - The king was drinking himself into drunkenness when he was assassinated

14) 1 Kings 20:12-21 - Ben-Hadad and 32 other kings were drinking when they were attacked and defeated by the Israelites.

15) Esther 1:5-12 - The king gave each one all the drink he wanted. The king was intoxicated when he commanded the queen to come.

16) Psalm 75:8 - The Lord's anger is pictured as mixed wine poured out and drunk by the wicked.

17) Proverbs 4:17 - Alcoholic drink is called the wine of violence.

18) Proverbs 20:1 - Wine is a mocker, strong drink is raging.

19) Proverbs 23:19-20 - A wise person will not be among the drinkers of alcoholic beverages.

20) Proverbs 23:21 - Drunkenness causes poverty.

21) Proverbs 23:29-30 - Drinking causes woe, sorrow, fighting, babbling, wounds without cause and red eyes.

22) Proverbs 23:31 - God instructs us not to look at intoxicating drinks.

23) Proverbs 23:32 - Alcoholic drinks bite like a serpent, sting like an adder.

24) Proverbs 23:33 - Alcohol causes the drinker to have

strange and adulterous thoughts, produces willfulness, and prevents reformation.

25) Proverbs 23:34 - Alcohol makes the drinker unstable

26) Proverbs 23:35 - Alcohol makes the drinker insensitive to pain so he does not perceive it as a warning. Alcohol is habit forming.

27) Proverb 31:4-5 - Kings, Princes, and others who rule and judge must not drink alcohol. Alcohol perverts good judgment.

28) Proverbs 31:6-7 - Strong drink could be given to those about to perish or those in pain. Better anesthetics are available today.

29) Ecclesiastes 2:3 - The king tried everything, including intoxicating drink, to see if it satisfied. It did not. (Ecclesiastes 12:8)

30) Ecclesiastes 10:17 - A land is blessed when its leaders do not drink.

31) Isaiah 5:11-12 - Woe to those who get up early to drink and stay up late at night to get drunk.

32) Isaiah 5:22 - Woe to "champion" drinkers and "experts" at mixing drinks.

33) Isaiah 19:14 - Drunken   men stagger in their vomit.

34) Isaiah 22:12-13 - The Israelites choose to drink; their future looks hopeless to them.

35) Isaiah 24:9 - Drinkers cannot escape the consequences when God judges.

36) Isaiah 28:1 - God pronounces woe on the drunkards of Ephraim.

37) Isaiah 28:3 - Proud drunkards shall be trodden down.

38) Isaiah 28:7 - Priests and prophets stagger and reel from beer and wine, err in vision, and stumble in judgment.

39) Isaiah 28:8 - Drinkers' tables are covered with vomit and filth.

40) Isaiah 56:9-12 - Drinkers seek their own gain and expect tomorrow to be just like today.

41) Jeremiah 35:2-14 - The Rechabites drank no grape juice or intoxicating wine and were blessed.

42) Ezekiel 44:21 - Again God instructed the priests not to drink wine.

43) Daniel 1:5-17 - Daniel refused the king's intoxicating wine and was blessed for it along with his abstaining friends.

44) Daniel 5:1 - Belshazzar, ruler of Babylon; led his people in drinking.

45) Daniel 5:2-3 - The king, along with his nobles, wives, and concubines, drank from the goblets which had been taken from God's temple.

46) Daniel 5:4 - Drinking wine was combined with praising false gods.

47) Daniel 5:23 - God sent word to Belshazzar that punishment would be swift for the evil he had committed.

48) Hosea 4:11 - Intoxicating wine takes away intelligence.

49) Hosea 7:5 - God reproves princes for drinking.

50) Joel 1:5 - Drunkards awake to see God's judgment.

51) Joel 3:3 - The enemy is judged for selling girls for wine.

52) Amos 2:8 - Unrighteous acts of Israel included the drinking of wine which had been taken for the payment of fines.

53) Amos 2:12 - Israel is condemned for forcing Nazarites to drink wine.

54) Micah 2:11 - Israelites are eager to follow false teachers who prophesy plenty of intoxicating drinks.

55) Nahum 1:10 - The drunkards of Nineveh will be destroyed by God.

56) Habakkuk 2:5 - A man is betrayed by wine.

57) Habakkuk 2:15 - Woe to him that gives his neighbor drink.

58) Habakkuk 2:16 - Drinking leads to shame.

59) Matthew 24:48-51 - A drinking servant is unprepared for his Lord's return.

60) Luke 1:15 - John the Baptist drank neither grape juice nor wine.

61) Luke 12:45 - Christ warned against drunkenness.

62) Luke 21:34 - Drunkenness will cause a person not to be ready for the Lord's return.

63) Romans 13:13 - Do not walk in drunkenness or immorality.

64) Romans 14:21 - Do not do anything that will hurt your testimony as a believer.

65) 1 Corinthians 5:11 - If a Christian brother is a drinker, do not associate with him.

66) 1 Corinthians 6:10 - Drunkards will not inherit the kingdom of God

67) Galatians 5:21 - Acts of the sinful nature, such as drunkenness, will prohibit a person from inheriting the kingdom of God.

68) Ephesians 5:18 - In contrast to being drunk with wine, the believer is to be filled with the Spirit.

69) 1 Thessalonians 5:6-7 - Christians are to be alert and self-controlled, belonging to the day. Drunkards belong to the night and darkness.

70) 1 Timothy 3:2-3 - Bishops (elders) are to be temperate, sober, and not near any wine.

71) 1 Timothy 3:8 - Deacons are to be worthy of respect and not drinkers.

72) 1 Timothy 3:11 - Deacons' wives are to be temperate and sober.

73) Titus 1:7-8 - An overseer is to be disciplined.

74) Titus 2:2-3 - The older men and older women of the church are to be temperate and not addicted to wine.

75) 1 Peter 4:3-4 - The past life of drunkenness and carousing has no place in the Christian's life.

Reasons not do drink

If you are not convinced yet, here are some other, more specific scriptural matters to consider.

It is a stumbling block.

> *1 Cor. 8:* *"⁹ But beware lest somehow this liberty of yours become a stumbling block to those who are weak. ¹⁰ For if anyone sees you who have knowledge eating in an idol's temple, will not the conscience of him who is weak be emboldened to eat those things offered to idols? ¹¹ And because of your knowledge shall the weak brother perish, for whom Christ died? ¹² But when you thus sin against the brethren, and wound their weak conscience, you sin against Christ.¹³ Therefore, if food makes my brother stumble, I will never again eat meat, lest I make my brother stumble."*

> *Romans 14:* *"²¹ It is good neither to eat meat nor drink wine nor do anything by which your brother stumbles or is offended or is made weak."*

It could be that the person that you cause to stumble might be your son or daughter. I wonder what their tolerance for alcohol might be.

Drinking alcohol does not glorifying God

1 Cor 6: "²⁰ For you were bought at a price; therefore glorify God in your body[c] and in your spirit, which are God's."

1 Cor 10: " ³¹ Therefore, whether you eat or drink, or whatever you do, do all to the glory of God."

It is a slippery slope

Prov. 23: "²⁹ Who has woe? Who has sorrow? Who has contentions? Who has complaints? Who has wounds without cause? Who has redness of eyes?"

None of those things sound pleasant to me.

"³⁰ Those who linger long at the wine, Those who go in search of mixed wine."

"Linger long?" What is your tolerance for alcohol? It might be better not to know.

"³¹ Do not look on the wine when it is red, When it sparkles in the cup, When it swirls around smoothly;"

Don't look at it.

"32 At the last it bites like a serpent, And stings like a viper."

It is poisonous.

"33 Your eyes will see strange things,"

It perverts your thinking.

"And your heart will utter perverse things."

It loosens the tongue.

"34 Yes, you will be like one who lies down in the midst of the sea, Or like one who lies at the top of the mast, saying:"

It loosens your equilibrium.

35 "They have struck me, but I was not hurt; They have beaten me, but I did not feel it."

It causes personal injury.

"When shall I awake, that I may seek another drink?"

It's addictive.

Self justification for believers to drink

If you're looking for permission to drink alcohol, you can't use the Bible. The wine in the Bible has no similarity to today's wine. But it's easy enough to justify. Simply repeat these words, "I don't care. I like it."

The Homosexual Discussion

As I write this paper, I am one day away from the supreme court of the United States making a landmark decision regarding homosexuality. Within the American moral landscape, this matter has become a very hot issue. At one point, within our American history, homosexuality (sodomy) was illegal in every state. In recent years, the pendulum has swung completely in the other direction and it is now *legal* in every state. The subject has become a political football that drives our elections and continues to divide our nation. Within the Christian world, the dialogue even divides supposed followers of Jesus. Some denominations tolerate and even embrace the idea, while others are vehemently opposed to the practice. The purpose of this paper is to cover the issue from the Biblical prospective, discuss the typical conversation, and approach what our attitudes and discussions should be.

The Scripture

The biblical narrative and history of the subject is unquestionably opposed to the behavior. The very first mention of homosexuality is found in Genesis chapter 13.

> Genesis 13 *"¹⁰And Lot lifted his eyes and saw all the plain of Jordan, that it was well watered*

everywhere (before the LORD destroyed Sodom and Gomorrah) like the garden of the LORD, like the land of Egypt as you go toward Zoar. [11] Then Lot chose for himself all the plain of Jordan, and Lot journeyed east. And they separated from each other. [12] Abram dwelt in the land of Canaan, and Lot dwelt in the cities of the plain and pitched his tent even as far as Sodom. [13] But the men of Sodom were exceedingly wicked and sinful against the LORD."

The men of Sodom were deemed to be "exceedingly wicked" by God, even before we were told why God considered them wicked. Today, we know the term "sodomy", which we link back to the men of Sodom. By definition, sodomy is oral or anal sex between persons of the same sex. In the national discourse, one can track the moral decline of America, as each state, one by one, repealed the state laws to permit sodomy. The country gradually went from agreeing with God's assessment of sodomy as "exceedingly wicked" to, morally acceptable.

In Genesis 19, we learn of the story of Sodom and Gomorrah. In the chapter before, 18, God let it be known to Abraham that He would destroy Sodom and Gomorrah, because of the exceeding wickedness. The angels of the Lord visited Lot in Sodom and became the object of the carnal lust of the men of Sodom. They wanted to commit sodomy with them. As a result, the men were struck blind by God to prevent them from committing such an abominable act.

> *Genesis 19: "⁴ Now before they lay down, the men of the city, the men of Sodom, both old and young, all the people from every quarter, surrounded the house. ⁵ And they called to Lot and said to him, "Where are the men who came to you tonight? Bring them out to us that we may know them carnally."*

> *⁶ So Lot went out to them through the doorway, shut the door behind him, ⁷ and said, "Please, my brethren, do not do so wickedly! ⁸ See now, I have two daughters who have not known a man; please, let me bring them out to you, and you may do to them as you wish; only do nothing to these men, since this is the reason they have come under the shadow of my roof."*

> *⁹ And they said, "Stand back!" Then they said, "This one came in to stay here, and he keeps acting as a judge; now we will deal worse with you than with them." So they pressed hard against the man Lot, and came near to break down the door. ¹⁰ But the men reached out their hands and*

pulled Lot into the house with them, and shut the door. [11] And they struck the men who were at the doorway of the house with blindness, both small and great, so that they became weary trying to find the door."

It seems unfathomable that such a thing would happen but, according to the biblical record, it happened. Shortly thereafter, as a result of their horrible sin, God destroyed the two cities. In the discipline of biblical interpretation, the first mention of *anything* reflects God's attitude toward that experience. Righteous indignation is Gods' attitude toward sodomy.

In Leviticus 18, God lays down the law regarding morality. He covers many situations that he forbids, regarding sexual deviation. One of those prohibitions is sex between parties of the same sex.

Leviticus 18: "[22]You shall not lie with a male as with a woman. It is an abomination."

With God, morality is nothing new. It is not a new notion designed to with-hold pleasure from mankind. Morality is morality. It existed in Abrahams' day, it existed in Moses' day, when he wrote Leviticus, and it exists in our day. God forbids sodomy.

Apparently, many people throughout history have tried to satisfy their sexual appetites with members of the same sex. In the book of Romans, in the New Testament, chapter 1, we find an interesting narrative. In verses 18 through 23, we are told that, historically, people who choose to ignore God, and even deny that God exists, are subject to God with-holding His righteous influence from their lives. The result of this withdrawal is that "mankind" sinks to his basest level of morality.

> Romans 1: "24 Therefore God also gave them up to uncleanness, in the lusts of their hearts, to dishonor their bodies among themselves, 25 who exchanged the truth of God for the lie, and worshiped and served the creature rather than the Creator, who is blessed forever. Amen.

> 26 For this reason God gave them up to vile passions. For even their women exchanged the natural use for what is against nature. 27 Likewise also the men, leaving the natural use of the woman, burned in their lust for one another, men with men committing what is shameful, and receiving in themselves the penalty of their error which was due.

> 28 And even as they did not like to retain God in their knowledge, God gave them over to a

debased mind, to do those things which are not fitting.."

I can't help but wonder how much of our national moral condition can be linked to eliminating God from our public forum and our national conversation. Today we kill unborn babies. In our lingo it is called choice or simply the right of women. It's interesting to me that this kind of murder can be linked to the above scripture. It's all about sex. Women have a great choice, but it should be made before a child is conceived. Sex drives our moral conscience. The scriptural withdrawal mentioned above is certainly at the personal level, but I fear that it is also at the national level. God has clearly with-held His righteous influence and we, nationally, have clearly sunk to our basest of selfish instincts.

The Argument

The homosexual community tries extremely hard to justify their behavior. I'm reminded of a lawyer in Scripture that asked Jesus questions about eternal life.

> *Luke 10: "25 And behold, a certain lawyer stood up and tested Him, saying, "Teacher, what shall I do to inherit eternal life?" 26 He said to him, "What is written in the law? What is your reading of it?" 27 So he answered and said, "You shall love the LORD your God with all your*

heart, with all your soul, with all your strength, and with all your mind,' and 'your neighbor as yourself.' 28 And He said to him, "You have answered rightly; do this and you will live." 29 But he, wanting to justify himself, said to Jesus, "And who is my neighbor?"

The passage is clear that he was trying to "justify" himself. He wasn't interested in the truth, he wanted to do his own thing, think his own way, make his life seem right to himself and not have to answer to the authority of God or Scripture. Of course, Jesus knew his heart. He knew that his question was not a question from a person seeking truth. The story that ensued was designed to break down the man's personal, self-serving beliefs. Self-serving beliefs are the most common way that people have of avoiding accountability and guilt.

Being educated in counseling, I recognize, through a persons' conversation, that he has insecurities. People with insecurities often criticize others and try to gain allies to their point of view. People who are secure in their lives generally don't care what others think about them. It seems to me that the "evangelistic" fervor, of the gay community, is an outcry for acceptance spawned by uncertainty. The arguments for acceptance do not make sense to me.

"I was born gay" one might say - "I have no choice." It is certain, through scripture, that we are all born sinners. We all have a propensity to do that which satisfies ourselves. Anyone, who has every seen a small child, knows that their only interest is *themselves*. They have to *learn* to share. They have to learn not to scream and cry to get their own way. They have to learn to eat their vegetables and not candy. They have to learn not to take things that are not theirs. In short, they have to learn personal discipline in order to not be self-serving. Later, we make choices. Some people choose to steal. Some people choose to drink alcohol. Some people choose to be sexually active at an early age. Some people choose to take drugs. Some even kill other people to get what they want. Regardless of how a man *feels* about his sexuality, at some point a clear choice is made to insert his penis into another mans' rectum – a place where e coli bacteria resides. This is hardly what God intended when He created rectums. (Sorry for being so graphic, it needs to be said)

"I can't help who I fall in love with", is another idea that I find implausible. Can I live in Florida and "fall" into love with a person that I have never seen, in China? Do you even know what love is? Do you know how love works? Lust should never be confused with love, even if you experience the most "amazing sex ever." What if a man decides that he "loves" adolescence boys? Does the argument work in that case? Absurd!

254

Politically Correct

One should never forget the influence of Satan in society. I'm afraid that he is smarter than us all. He knows how to subtly attack us without it being obvious. He backs into ideas and draws us in, playing on our own lusts. He offered Eve knowledge. Being knowledgeable sounds harmless enough, doesn't it? Now some of the smartest people in our country have set the definition for what is "correct." The week that I am writing this article, the supreme court of America has said directly, that if you view homosexuality through a moral lens, you are a bigot. I'm afraid that those who lead our national conversation have "bitten" on Satan's apple.

The word prejudice has become a poison to our society. In my opinion, everyone is prejudice about something, but we are not allowed to say so. I almost feel that the word prejudice is interchangeable with the word preference. I am clearly prejudiced against moral evils. I, however, am not smart enough to define "moral evil." My standard, for such definitions, is the Bible. It takes the guesswork out of defining a moral direction. Political correctness is a poison apple. It prevents many people from saying what they actually think.

Christian Dialogue

Make no assumption when you hear the word Christian. The word has, generally, become meaningless. Having said that, how useful is the discussion from the "Christian" community? I get nervous when a believer says that "they know where I stand." It sounds confrontational to me. *Confrontation rarely conveniences!*

Some "Christians" *accept* the practice of homosexuality and even promote ministers who are homosexual. The justifications include: promoting grace, tolerance, open mindedness, Old Testament vs. New Testament, law vs. grace and a politically correct agenda.

Other "believers" are very vocal *against* homosexuality. They, of course, are labeled homophobes. Homophobia is a word that has been devised, as a criticism, for anyone opposing this sexual deviance. Phobia is a fear of something. The implication is that people who oppose homosexuality, fear homosexuals. The subject of morality is not considered.

I find it troublesome that some of the most *vocal* "Christians" use cleaver, demeaning, sound-bites like "God hates fags" and "God didn't create Adam and Steve." I'm afraid that this kind of talk hurts the cause of morality and does not help. It plays into the shrill name calling.

Pick Your Spots

Believers – followers of Jesus – are instructed in Scripture to spread the Gospel – the good   news.

Matthew 28: "¹⁹ Go therefore¹ and make disciples
of all the nations, baptizing them in the name of
the Father and of the Son and of the Holy
Spirit, ²⁰ teaching them to observe all things that I
have commanded you; and lo, 1 am with you
always, even to the end of the age." Amen"

They are also asked to be salt and light, (preserving, making a difference and enlightening), in the world.

Matthew 5: "¹³ "You are the salt of the earth; but
if the salt loses its flavor, how shall it be
seasoned? It is then good for nothing but to be
thrown out and trampled underfoot by men.

¹⁴ "You are the light of the world. A city that is set
on a hill cannot be hidden. ¹⁵ Nor do they light a
lamp and put it under a basket, but on a lamp-
stand, and it gives light to all who are in the
house. ¹⁶ Let your light so shine before men, that
they may see your good works and glorify your
Father in heaven."

By blending these two ideas together, there seems to be a way of affecting the world, without the shrill political and moral outrage that has become our national dialogue – we should **spread** the good news of Jesus and **live** the results of following Him.

The purpose of church is to help believers have clean lives and hearts, and an understanding of the mission.

> *Ephesians 4: "[11] And He Himself gave some to be apostles, some prophets, some evangelists, and some pastors and teachers, [12] for the equipping of the saints for the work of ministry, for the edifying of the body of Christ, [13] till we all come to the unity of the faith and of the knowledge of the Son of God, to a perfect man, to the measure of the stature of the fullness of Christ; [14] that we should no longer be children, tossed to and fro and carried about with every wind of doctrine, by the trickery of men, in the cunning craftiness of deceitful plotting, [15] but, speaking the truth in love, may grow up in all things into Him who is the head—Christ— [16] from whom the whole body, joined and knit together by what every joint supplies, according to the effective working by which every part does its share, causes growth of the body for the edifying of itself in love."*

Notice that a key ingredient in this passage is "love." The word is mentioned twice, and includes the ideas of "speaking" in love, and "growing together" in love. It paints a beautiful picture. Believers should rail against sin, but it should be done in the confines of the church, where the believers are learning and being "perfected." Railing should somehow be tempered with love so that the message is not hateful. Hateful language does not breed love.

The Perspective

The best way to change society is to change the hearts of its people. If we change a person's morality and behavior without changing his heart, we create a Pharisee. Jesus had some things to say about the Pharisees and their outward righteousness.

> *Matthew 23: [27] "Woe to you, scribes and Pharisees, hypocrites! For you are like whitewashed tombs which indeed appear beautiful outwardly, but inside are full of dead men's bones and all uncleanness. [28] Even so you also outwardly appear righteous to men, but inside you are full of hypocrisy and lawlessness."*

Jesus gave some explicit instructions about changing society.

> *Matthew 23: [25] "Woe to you, scribes and Pharisees, hypocrites! For you cleanse the outside of the cup and dish, but inside they are full of extortion and self-indulgence. [26] Blind Pharisee, first cleanse the inside of the cup and dish, that the outside of them may be clean also."*

When Christians publically condemn specific sins, they are spitting into the wind. All it does is create controversy and makes the *real* message unintelligible. During the days of prohibition (non alcohol), Christians and preachers loudly protested the evils of alcohol. The temporary result was prohibition. It didn't take long for the law to be repealed because of unintended consequences – mob violence, secret bars, stills, murders, great costs for enforcement, and lost tax revenue. The outside was changed but not the inside, the hearts. We shouldn't *be* Pharisees *creating* Pharisees.

The Blurred Line

Christians are asked to "contend for the faith." Unfortunately, the most vocal of the believers present themselves in a very contentious manner. It is difficult to articulate a moral standard without the shrill passion that makes believers look bigoted. We seem to fall into the same loud wrangling pattern that is used by amoral, self-justifying people. I am astonished when homosexuals take to the streets in "gay pride" demonstrations. I certainly feel that followers of Jesus cannot afford that kind of visible display, if indeed we want to win homosexuals, (or anyone for that matter).

How then should we protest? How can we influence society? Don't we have a responsibility, as a citizen, to affect the mores of society? We are reminded that we "wrestle not against flesh and blood." Our struggle is spiritual and our best defense may, in fact, be a good spiritual offense. Our spiritual struggle can be won in the hearts of the lost, one soul at a time. Several other steps that can help include:

1) Become evangelistic avoiding controversy.

2) Use political influence and keep the discussion impersonal.

3) Avoid passionate sound bites which ultimately inflame the matter.

4) Help other believers gain public office.

5) Pastors should properly disciple believers to be loving people.

If you want to know what your personal attitude should be, act as if you just found out that your son or daughter just announced their homosexuality. It is my observation that parents who find out such news have a serious change of heart, overnight. If we as believers behave "that" way with others, we may actually do some good.

The Conclusion

Whose sin is greater, the homosexuals or the believers who drive them away? Have we failed to be "salt and light?" Do we bare some of the responsibility for the moral condition of America?

My opinion is that, Christians, who are interested in personal evangelism, are much more sensitive in their speech than those who only want to criticize. That is the sin of the Pharisees. In the 1970's, when men began to let their hair grow as a "protest" against authority, they were met with much opposition by churches and pastors. I remember one acquaintance of mine that was vehemently vocal about the issue. Later, he became a pastor charged with winning and discipling the very people he spoke against. One day, I saw him with one of his new converts. The convert had long hair. In my heart, I smiled at the change in a person who "generally" was opposed to something but had to temper his attitude when it became personal.

Adopt this mind-set and see if it doesn't work. *You can't scale a fish before you get him into the boat.*

Shorts

I'm not satisfied yet! There are many more ideas that still bother me. Without trying too hard to solve them, here are a few.

Jewishness

This may be a new word, but it needs some discussion. In today's Christian culture, there seems to be a movement *back* to our Jewish roots. Classes are being conducted by Jewish believers; churches are observing traditional Jewish celebrations and even inviting Rabbis to come speak to the Christian congregation. I am not fully informed, but have some thoughts about the movement.

> 1) I wish that the words Jewish and Christian did not exist. What would our faith community look like without divisions?

> 2) I am not Jewish. Should I observe Jewish tradition? Should Jewish men still be circumcised whether they are believers or not?

> 3) Should I observe the Sabbath? The Sabbath commandment is the only one of the Ten Commandments that is not repeated in the New Testament.

4) Hasn't the question of being Jewish been asked and answered in Acts chapter 15 by the early Jewish followers of Jesus as the Messiah?

5) I sense another distraction. The Great Commission seems fairly plain. It doesn't require much interpretation or study to understand the issue. *The lost world needs saving.* Why do you suppose that believers – followers of Jesus – would rather go to yet ANOTHER Bible study instead of make an investment in souls? It's puzzling to me.

Legalism

The term was originally used to describe Jewish converts who wanted to make keeping Jewish tradition a requirement for the lost to be saved. Once again, the matter was discussed at the council in Jerusalem in Acts 15, and rejected. The church at Galatia was also guilty of trying to combine faith with tradition as a requirement for salvation. That is legalism.

Today, however, the term has changed radically. It seems to be used whenever a church holds high standards for the adherence of their congregation. Some pastors preach that the women in their church should present themselves in modest apparel. That doesn't seem out of line to me because the Bible teaches such a thing.

These pastors are called legalists. Some pastors preach that certain habits that harm the body should be avoided. That also seems scriptural to me. Once again these pastors are called legalists.

Some churches may go overboard, but it should be pointed out that we live in America and people have choices. No-one is required to go to these churches. Perhaps more pastors should raise the bar a bit for believers and preach a higher moral standard. In some cases, it's hard to distinguish church goers from those who attending a rock concert. If the *church* does not preach a higher standard, who will? It's called discipleship.

I think that the term "legalism" has turned into a criticism for people who have a higher standard than you have. Perhaps the "church" should do less criticizing and more evangelizing.

Context, context, context

One big issue within the Christian community is the misuse of Scripture. Sadly, many believers use Scripture to make themselves feel good when life gets hard. The following verses seem to be overused and taken out of context in their use.

Phil. 4:13 "I can do all things through Christ who strengthens me."

Paul is talking about being able to live a meager lifestyle. I have never heard this verse quoted from anyone trying to learn to live within a meager lifestyle. It is mostly quoted when life's struggles get tough. I entered a room one day and heard a woman spouting off saying "my Bible tells me that God will take care of me." I didn't know anyone in the room but found myself telling her "that's what John the Baptist said right before he had his head cut off." Think about it.

Phil. 4:19 "And my God shall supply all your need according to His riches in glory by Christ Jesus."

This is Paul telling the church at Philippi, who had helped him financially, that God apparently could trust them with resources. They seemed to have their priorities right. The promise was to a church that had helped a missionary. The "need" of a church like that is different from a church that wants new carpet. Think about it.

2 Chronicles 7:14 "if My people who are called by My name will humble themselves, and pray and seek My face, and turn from their wicked ways, then I will hear from heaven, and will forgive their sin and heal their land."

In the verses immediately preceding verse 14, God had warned the nation of Israel that if they went into sin, God would curse their land. If they repented then God would heal their land. America is not God's chosen people. Christians do not bear His name, Israel (prince of God). Our land has never been cursed because America has turned from Him, (thank God). America is deep in sin today. We kill babies. Alcohol flows like a river. The sins of Sodom have become commonplace. We don't seem to have any moral compass anymore, and yet our land is not cursed. We may be able to put together Scripture that calls for personal repentance, but that will not turn the nation to God. It never has. Think about it.

Luke 6:38 "Give, and it will be given to you: good measure, pressed down, shaken together, and running over will be put into your bosom. For with the same measure that you use, it will be measured back to you."

How many times have you heard this Scripture quoted just before the offering was taken in church? The context is not about money and says nothing about putting money into the offering plate. The context is from the Sermon on the Mount where Jesus is talking to the people about their inner life. He is talking about relationship matters and how to interact with others. The subject is a giving spirit – being generous with your fellow man. One may apply this concept when the church takes the offering, but that is not the context. Think about it.

Jeremiah 29:11 "For I know the thoughts that I think toward you, says the LORD, thoughts of peace and not of evil, to give you a future and a hope."

Most believers can quote this verse. It is used to encourage individuals that something good is going to happen to them, regardless of their present circumstances. It also creates more doctrine than is intended. I find it interesting that no-one can quote Jeremiah 29:10. Spoken to Israel, specifically the capitol city of Jerusalem, from the southern kingdom, Judah, God said *"For thus says the LORD: After seventy years are completed at Babylon, I will visit you and perform My good word toward you, and cause you to return to this place."* Unfortunately for the individuals in the southern kingdom, 80% of them were killed during the invasion from Babylon. The rest of the people were taken captive to Babylon where the majority of them died before the seventy years ended.

Jeremiah 29:11 was a providential statement made by God regarding the subsequent 3000 years for the *nation* of Israel. It did not impact *individuals*. It was a statement made to the nation of Israel regarding its future. Furthermore, the verse does not mean that God has a plan for *you* that will make *you* feel good in the future. At the personal level, our ultimate hope is that those who have accepted Jesus as his Savior will spend eternity with Him. You may be martyred to get there, but it will feel good in the *next* life. Think about it.

Romans 8:28 "And we know that all things work together for good to those who love God, to those who are the called according to His purpose."

Beware! This verse is full of caveats. What are "all things?" What is "good?" Do all believers "love God?" Who is "called?" What is "His purpose?" How many believers fit into this verse? Do you? Is pain ever good? Think about it.

James 4:2 "...you do not have because you do not ask."

Have you ever quoted this verse when discussing prayer? I have. However, the verse before and the first part of this verse discusses relationship matters and hindrances to good relationships – greed, lust, covetousness, strife, murder, frustration, war and fighting. This is hardly a prayer Scripture. Think about it.

Take courage

There are some great verses of Scripture that can speak to us, which were actually meant for us. Here are a few.

Joshua 1:8 "This Book of the Law shall not depart from your mouth, but you shall meditate in it day and night, that you may observe to do according to all that is written in it. For then you will make your way prosperous, and then you will have good success."

Psalm 1:1-3 "Blessed is the man who walks not in the counsel of the ungodly, Nor stands in the path of sinners, Nor sits in the seat of the scornful; ² But his delight is in the law of the LORD, And in His law he meditates day and night. ³ He shall be like a tree Planted by the rivers of water, That brings forth its fruit in its season, Whose leaf also shall not wither; And whatever he does shall prosper."

Proverbs 3:5-6 "Trust in the LORD with all your heart, And lean not on your own understanding; ⁶ In all your ways acknowledge Him, And He shall direct your paths."

Matt 5:16 " Let your light so shine before men, that they may see your good works and glorify your Father in heaven."

Matt. 6:19-21 "Do not lay up for yourselves treasures on earth, where moth and rust destroy and where thieves break in and steal; ²⁰ but lay up for yourselves treasures in heaven, where neither moth nor rust destroys and where thieves do not break in and steal."

Matt. 6:24 "No one can serve two masters; for either he will hate the one and love the other, or else he will be loyal to the one and despise the other. You cannot serve God and mammon."

Matt. 6:25-26 "Therefore 1 say to you, do not worry about your life, what you will eat or what you will drink; nor about your body, what you will put on. Is not life more than food and the body more than clothing? 26 Look at the birds of the air, for they neither sow nor reap nor gather into barns; yet your heavenly Father feeds them. Are you not of more value than they?"

Matt. 11:28-29 "Come to Me, all you who labor and are heavy laden, and 1 will give you rest. 29 Take My yoke upon you and learn from Me, for 1 am gentle and lowly in heart, and you will find rest for your souls."

John 3:16 "For God so loved the world that He gave His only begotten Son, that whoever believes in Him should not perish but have everlasting life."

Acts 1:8 "But you shall receive power when the Holy Spirit has come upon you; and you shall be witnesses to Me in Jerusalem, and in all Judea and Samaria, and to the end of the earth."

Romans 10:9-10 "that if you confess with your mouth the Lord Jesus and believe in your heart that God has raised Him from the dead, you will be saved. ¹⁰ For with the heart one believes unto righteousness, and with the mouth confession is made unto salvation."

Romans 10:13 "For "whoever calls on the name of the LORD shall be saved."

Ephesians 3:20 "Now to Him who is able to do exceedingly abundantly above all that we ask or think, according to the power that works in us, ²¹ to Him be glory in the church by Christ Jesus to all generations, forever and ever."

Philippians 4:6-7 "Be anxious for nothing, but in everything by prayer and supplication, with thanksgiving, let your requests be made known to God; ⁷ and the peace of God, which surpasses all understanding, will guard your hearts and minds through Christ Jesus."

Hebrews 4:15 "For we do not have a High Priest who cannot sympathize with our weaknesses, but was in all points tempted as we are, yet without sin. ¹⁶ Let us therefore come boldly to the throne of grace that we may obtain mercy and find grace to help in time of need."

Discipleship – when is it enough?

Once a person accepts Jesus as his Savior, he is to be trained in the Scripture and purpose of the Gospel. The purpose of the Gospel is to reach the world for Jesus. I fear that we have created a Christian culture of people stuck in study. New believers go to class or church and *soak* in the Word. At some point they are supposed to begin sharing their faith with the lost world – their lost world.

Perhaps you too have noticed that most believers NEVER do that. How much discipleship is enough to begin sharing your faith? Perhaps it should be the *first* thing that you do, not the last. In John chapter 4, after Jesus had His encounter with the woman at the well, the FIRST thing that she did was go back to the town and share her new found faith with the towns people. Many believed. We have it backwards!

The latest thing

American Christianity has evolved into an event driven life. It is remarkable that believers seem to be constantly waiting for the "latest thing" – the latest book, the latest video, the latest singing group, the latest slogan, the latest simulcast, the latest evangelist, the latest conference. People would rather take a class on prophecy, measure their spiritual gifts or Google Bible studies. The Great Commission takes work. It takes focus. It takes intentionality. It almost seems that Christians are looking for a way out of building relationships for the purpose of advancing the Kingdom.

None of these things are, in themselves, bad. Who would deny that anyone involving themselves in such activities are good people? Is it a problem that Christians get involved in "good" things, but leave off the "best" thing – reaching the lost world? Could it be that Satan is involved in distracting people away from the "mission?" In the Garden of Eden, Satan offered Eve *knowledge*. Certainly *knowledge* is not a bad thing, is it? We are told to avoid distractions in Hebrews 12:1

> *"……..let us lay aside every weight, and the sin which so easily ensnares us, and let us run with endurance the race that is set before us"*

The "weight" mentioned above is not sin. Sin is mentioned as being something separate from "weight." Perhaps this knowledge that we are seeking has become weights which keep us from running the race efficiently and effectively.

Seek knowledge to *assist* in the mission and not to *replace* the mission.

Know this!

"A ship in a harbor is safe, but that is not the purpose of ships." –
Author unknown

The purpose of a disciple is to make disciples.